생활 속의 참선수행 Practice In Daily Life ⑪

Inherent Connections:
Children, Parents, and the Dharma all around us

진짜 통하게 되면

진짜 통하게 되면
대행큰스님 법문
생활 속의 참선수행 ⑪ / 한영합본

발행일	2016년 5월 초판 1쇄
	2016년 8월 초판 2쇄
영문번역	한마음국제문화원
표지디자인	박수연
편집	한마음국제문화원
발행	한마음출판사
출판등록	384-2000-000010
전화	031-470-3175
팩스	031-470-3209
이메일	onemind@hanmaum.org

© 2016(재)한마음선원
본 출판물은 저작권법에 의하여 보호를 받는 저작물이므로
무단 복제와 무단 전재를 할 수 없습니다.

Inherent Connections:
Children, Parents, and the Dharma all around us
Practice in Daily Life ⑪ / Bilingual, Korean · English
Dharma Talks by Seon Master Daehaeng

First Edition First Print: May 2016
First Edition Second Print: August 2016
English Translation by
Hanmaum International Culture Institute
Edited by Hanmaum International Culture Institute
Cover Design by Su Yeon Park
Published by Hanmaum Publications
www.hanmaumbooks.org

© 2016 Hanmaum Seonwon Foundation
All rights reserved, including the right to reproduce
this work in any form.

Printed in the Republic of Korea

ISBN 978-89-91857-41-4 (04220) / 978-89-951830-0-7 (set)

국립중앙도서관 출판예정도서목록(CIP)

진짜 통하게 되면 = Inherent connections : children, parents and the Dharma all around us : 한영합본 / 대행큰스님 법문 ; 영문번역: 한마음국제문화원. -- [안양] : 한마음출판사, 2016
  p. ;   cm. -- (생활 속의 참선 수행 =Practice in daily life ; 11)

한영대역본임
ISBN 978-89-91857-41-4 04220 : US$6.00
ISBN 978-89-951830-0-7 (세트) 04220

설법[說法]
법문(불경)[法文]

225.2-KDC6
294.34-DDC23   CIP2016009842

A CIP catalogue record of the National Library of Korea for this book is available at the homepage of CIP(http://seoji.nl.go.kr) and Korean Library Information System Network(http://www.nl.go.kr/kolisnet). (CIP2016009842)

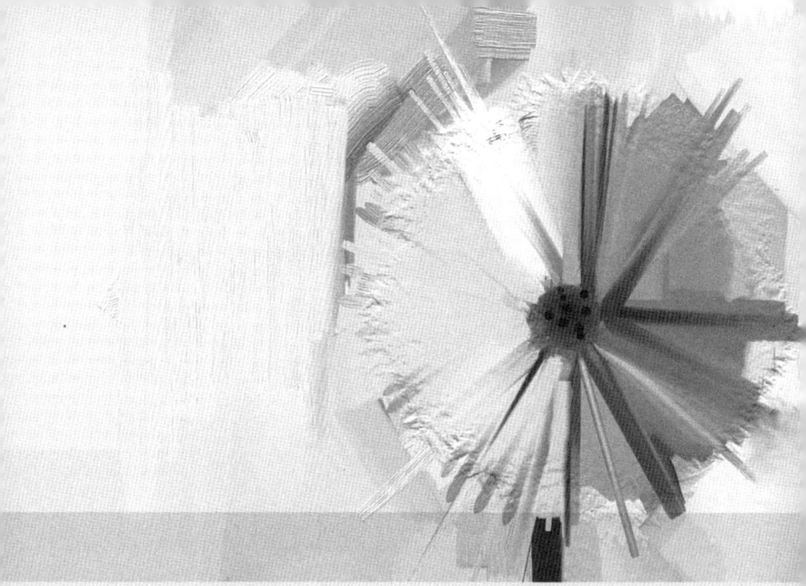

Inherent Connections:

Children, Parents, and the Dharma all around us

Seon Master Daehaeng

진짜 통하게 되면

대행큰스님 법문

한마음
hanmaum

...이렇게 **이심전심으로** 사랑과 자비, 의리를 가지고 가정을 이끌어 나가야지요.
이게, **부모의 참 사랑**입니다.

차 례

12 머리글

14 대행큰스님에 대하여

26 진짜 통하게 되면

...This is **truly loving** someone, this is the way to raise your family – **communicating directly through mind,** with love, generosity, and trust.

Contents

13 Foreword

15 About Daehaeng Kun Sunim

27 Inherent Connections:
Children, Parents, and the Dharma all around us

삼세가 둘 아니게 흐르니

흘러흘러 헤일 수 없는
겁劫을 지난 동안에
부모가 자식 되고
자식이 부모 되어
거듭거듭 형성됨을
이루 말로 다하랴.

과거생활 산 것대로
끼리끼리 인연되어
이 세상에 태어나서
한 철 살기 어려우나
일체가 내 부모 내 자식
아님 없거늘
어찌 끝없는 흐름에
평등 공법 아니랴.
평등 공법 아니랴.

Ceaselessly Flowing

Flowing and flowing,
endless eons of flowing,
parents becoming children,
children becoming parents,
changing their shapes over and over,
how can words describe all of this?

Gathering together
according to how we've lived in the past,
according to the karmic affinity we've created,
and being born into this world,
with so many hardships in just a single season.
Every being is my parent,
everyone is my child.
Oh, this endless flowing,
connected altogether and ceaselessly changing.

흘러흘러 헤일 수 없는

겁劫을 지난 동안에

거듭거듭 모습 바꿔

형성 될 때마다

과거생활 산 것대로

그 인과로 인해

몸 속에 유전되어

내 몸을 집 삼아

그 속에서 더불어 살며

안과 밖을 괴롭히는 생명들을

둘 아니게 조복 받아 공심이면

자유권을 자재 하는

평등공법 아니랴.

평등공법 아니랴.

-대행큰스님 게송 중에서

Flowing and flowing,
endless eons of flowing,
changing our shapes over and over,
each time according to our last life.
How we lived becomes our karma,
the process of cause and effect forms our genes.
This body is like a house,
with so many beings living here altogether.
Take all those lives that are bothering you,
whether they come from the inside or outside,
accept them non-dually,
make them one,
and watch them surrender.
Discover what it means to be truly free,
with the power that comes from being
connected altogether and ceaselessly changing.

— Daehaeng

머리글

대행큰스님이 지난 50여 년 동안 끊임없이 중생들에게 베풀어주신 수많은 법문이 있었지만, 핵심을 짚어내는 하나의 단어가 있다면, 그건 아마도 "참나"일 것입니다. 항상 나와 함께 있어서 보지 못하는 내 안의 진짜 나, 그 "참나"를 발견하여 당당하고 싱그럽게 살아가기를 바라는, 중생을 위한 스님의 간절한 바램은 이 한 편의 법문 속에도 여지없이 드러나 있습니다.

누구에게나 내면에는 만물만생을 다 먹여 살리고도 되남는 마음속 한 점의 불씨가 있습니다. 그 영원한 불씨를 찾아 광대무변한 마음법의 이치를 체득하여, 진정한 자유인으로서, 우주의 한 일원으로서 당당히 그 역할을 해나가길 바라는 대행큰스님의 간곡한 뜻이 이 법문을 통해 여러분 모두의 마음에 전해지길 바랍니다.

한마음국제문화원 일동 합장

Foreword

Over the last fifty years, Daehaeng Kun Sunim gave countless Dharma talks and teachings to beings without number, but if all those talks could be summed up into one word, it would be "true self."

This true essence has always been with us, yet remains unseen. Discover it for yourself, and in doing so, learn to live with courage, dignity, and joy. That all beings should awaken to this true essence is Daehaeng Kun Sunim's deepest wish. When you've tasted the purest and most refreshing spring water imaginable, you naturally want to share it with others.

Within us all is this seed, this spark that feeds and sustains each and every being. Discover this eternal spark and realize its profound and unlimited ability. If you can do this, you'll know what it means to truly be a free person, and you can fulfill the great role that is yours as a member of the whole universe.

With palms together,
The Hanmaum International Culture Institute

대행큰스님에 대하여

　대행큰스님께서는 여러 면에서 매우 보기 드문 선사(禪師)셨다. 무엇보다 선사라면 당연히 비구 스님을 떠올리는 전통 속에서 여성으로서 선사가 되셨으며, 비구 스님들을 제자로 두었던 유일한 비구니 스님이셨고, 노년층 여성이 주된 신도계층을 이루었던 한국 불교에 젊은 세대의 청장년층 남녀들을 대거 참여하게 만들어 한국불교에 새로운 풍격(風格)을 일으키는데 일조한 큰 스승이셨다. 또한 전통 비구니 강원과 비구니 종단에 대한 지속적인 지원을 펼치심으로써 비구니 승단을 발전시키는데 중추적인 역할을 하셨다.

　큰스님께서는 어느 누구나 마음수행을 통해 깨달을 수 있음을 강조하시며 삭발제자와 유발제자를 가리지 않고 법을 구하는 이들에게는 모두 똑같이 가르침을 주셨다.

　스님은 1927년 서울에서 태어나 일찍이 9세경에 자성을 밝히셨고 당신이 증득(證得)하신 바를 완성하기 위해 오랫동안 산중에서 수행하셨다. 훗날, 누더기가 다 된 해어진 옷을 걸치고 손에 주어지는 것만을 먹으며 지냈던 그 당시를 회상하며 스님은 의도적으로 고행을

About Daehaeng Kun Sunim

Daehaeng *Kun Sunim*[1] (1927-2012) was a rare teacher in Korea: a female *Seon(Zen)*[2] master, a nun whose students included monks as well as nuns, and a teacher who helped revitalize Korean Buddhism by dramatically increasing the participation of young people and men. She broke out of traditional models of spiritual practice to teach in such a way that allowed anyone to practice and awaken, making laypeople a particular focus of her efforts. At the same time, she was a major force for the advancement of *Bhikkunis*,[3] heavily supporting traditional nuns' colleges as well as the modern Bhikkuni Council of Korea.

---

1. Sunim / Kun Sunim: Sunim is the respectful title of address for a Buddhist monk or nun in Korea, and Kun Sunim is the title given to outstanding nuns or monks.

2. Seon(禪)(Chan, Zen)**:** Seon describes the unshakeable state where one has firm faith in their inherent foundation, their Buddha-nature, and so returns everything they encounter back to this fundamental mind. It also means letting go of "I," "me," and "mine" throughout one's daily life.

3. Bhikkunis: Female sunims who are fully ordained are called Bhikkuni(比丘尼) sunims, while male sunims who are fully ordained are called Bhikku(比丘) sunims. This can also be a polite way of indicating male or female sunims.

하고자 했던 것이 아니라 당신에게 주어진 환경이 그러했노라고, 또한 근본 불성자리에 일체를 맡기고 그 맡긴 일이 어떻게 작용하는지를 관하는 일에 완전히 몰두하고 있었기에 다른 것에는 신경을 쓸 틈이 없었노라고 말씀하셨다.

그 시절의 체험이 스님의 가르치는 방식을 형성하는데 깊은 영향을 미쳤다. 스님은 우리가 본래부터 어마어마한 잠재력을, 무궁무진한 에너지와 지혜를 가지고 있는데도 대부분이 그 역량을 알지 못해 끊임없이 많은 고통을 겪으며 살고 있음을 절실히 느끼며 안타까워하셨다. 우리들 각자 안에 존재하는 이 위대한 빛을 명백히 알고 있었기에, 스님은 본래부터 가지고 있는 근본자성(自性)인 참나를 믿고 의지해 살라 가르치셨고, 이 중요한 진리에서 벗어나는 그 어떤 것도 가르치기를 단호히 거부하셨다.

의도한 바는 아니셨지만, 스님은 매일매일의 일상 속에서 누구나 내면에 갖추어 가지고 있는 근본이자 진수(眞髓)인 참나와 진정으로 통할 수 있게 되었을 때 어떠한 일이 일어나는지를 역력히 보여 주셨다. 사람들은 스님 곁에 있을 때 자신들을 무한히 받아주고 품어주는 것만 같은, 말로 형언키 어려운 정밀(靜謐)한 기운을 느꼈고, 스님이 다른 사람들을 도와줄 때 드러내 보이는 깊은 법력 또한 목도하곤 하였다. 하지만 이 모든 일들은 당신

Born in Seoul, Korea, she awakened when she was around eight years old and spent the years that followed learning to put her understanding into practice. For years, she wandered the mountains of Korea, wearing ragged clothes and eating only what was at hand. Later, she explained that she hadn't been pursuing some type of asceticism; rather, she was just completely absorbed in entrusting everything to her fundamental *Buddha*[4] essence and observing how that affected her life.

Those years profoundly shaped Kun Sunim's later teaching style; she intimately knew the great potential, energy, and wisdom inherent within each of us, and recognized that most of the people she encountered suffered because they didn't realize this about themselves. Seeing clearly the great light in every individual, she taught people to rely upon this inherent foundation, and refused to teach anything that distracted from this most important truth.

Without any particular intention to do so, Daehaeng Kun Sunim demonstrated on a daily basis the freedom and ability that arises when

---

4. Buddha: In this text, "Buddha" and "Bodhisattva" are capitalized out of respect, because these represent the essence and function of the enlightened mind. "The Buddha" always refers to Sakyamuni Buddha.

자신을 돋보이게 하거나 과시하려 했던 게 아니었다. 사실 스님께서는 당신의 법력을 늘 감추려고 하셨다. 마음공부의 목적이 놀라운 능력을 갖게 되는 것이 아님에도 대중들이 그것에만 집착하게 되는 폐단을 우려하셨기 때문이었다.

 그렇지만 당신이 하신 모든 일을 통해, 우리가 내면에 있는 참나와 진정으로 하나가 되었을 때 그 능력과 자유로움이 어떤 것인지를 보여주셨다. 스님은 우리 모두가 근본을 통해 연결되어 있으므로 다 통할 수 있고, 그럼으로써 서로 깊이 이해 할 수 있다는 것을 보여주셨으며, 더 나아가 우리가 근본자리에서 일으키는 한 생각이 이 세상에 법이 되어 돌아갈 수 있다는 것도 보여주셨다.

 어떤 의미에서는 이 모든 일이 우리가 만물만생과 정말로 하나가 되었을 때 자연스레 부수적으로 나오는 것이라고 할 수 있다. 상대를 둘로 보거나 방해물로 여기는 마음이 사라졌을 때, 진정으로 모두와 조화롭게 흘러갈 수 있게 되었을 때 이 모든 일이 가능할 수 있게 되는 것이다. 이렇게 되면, 다가오는 상대가 누구든 별개의 존재로 느끼지 않게 된다. 그들이 또 다른 우리 자신들의 모습이기 때문이다. 일체가 둘이 아님을 뼛속 깊이 느끼는 사람이, 어찌 자신 앞에 닥친 인연을 나 몰라라 하고 등져 버릴 수 있겠는가?

we truly connect with this fundamental essence inherent within us. The sense of acceptance and connection people felt from being around her, as well as the abilities she manifested, weren't things she was trying to show off. In fact, she usually tried to hide them because people would tend to cling to these, without realizing that chasing after them cannot lead to either freedom or awakening.

Nonetheless, in her very life, in everything she did, she demonstrated the freedom and ability that arises when we truly connect with this very basic, fundamental essence that we all have – that we are. She showed that because we are all interconnected, we can deeply understand what's going on with others, and that the intentions we give rise to can manifest and function in the world.

All of these are in a sense side effects, things that arise naturally when we are truly one with everyone and thing around us. They happen because we are able to flow in harmony with our world, with no dualistic views or attachments to get in the way. At this point, other beings are not cut off from us; they are another shape of ourselves. Who, feeling this to their very bones, could turn their back on others?

스님은 중생들이 가지고 오는 어려운 문제나 상황들을 해결할 수 있도록 도와주셨으며, 이러한 스님의 자비로운 원력은 당신이 도시로 나와 본격적으로 대중들을 가르치기 이전에 이미 한국에서는 전설이 되어 있었다. 1950년대 말경, 치악산 상원사 근처 한 움막에서 수행차 몇년 간 머무르신 적이 있었는데, 그 소문을 듣고 전국에서 찾아오는 사람들이 끊이질 않았다. 차마 그들의 고통스런 호소를 내칠수가 없었던 스님은 일일이 그들의 말에 귀기울이며 마음을 다해 그들을 도와주셨다. 스님은 자비를 물 마른 웅덩이에서 죽어가는 물고기를 살리는 방생에 비유하셨다. 집세가 없어 셋집에서 쫓겨난 사람들에게 집을 마련해 주고, 학비가 없어서 학교를 마칠 수 없는 학생들에게 학비를 대주셨지만, 스님의 자비행(慈悲行)을 아는 사람은 손을 꼽을 정도밖에 되지 않았다.

그러나 문제를 해결해 주면 그때뿐 또 다른 문제가 닥쳐오면 속수무책이 되어 버리고 마는 사람들을 보며, 스님께서는 중생들이 자신의 문제를 스스로 해결하고 윤회(輪廻)[1]의 굴레에서

---

1. 윤회(輪廻): 산스크리트어의 삼사라(samsara)를 번역한 말로 쉼 없이 돈다는 생사의 바퀴를 뜻함. 다시 말해, 수레바퀴가 끊임없이 구르는 것과 같이, 중생이 번뇌와 업에 의하여 삼계(三界: 색계, 욕계, 무색계) 육도(六道: 지옥, 아귀, 축생, 아수라, 인간, 천상)라는 생사의 세계를 그치지 않고 돌고 도는 현상을 일컬음.

It was this deep compassion that made her a legend in Korea long before she formally started teaching. She was known for having the spiritual power to help people in all circumstances and with every kind of problem. She compared compassion to freeing a fish from a drying puddle, putting a homeless family into a home, or providing the school fees that would allow a student to finish high school. And when she did things like this, and much more, few knew that she was behind it.

Her compassion was also unconditional. She would offer what help she could to individuals and organizations, whether they be Christian or Buddhist, a private organization or governmental. She would help nun's temples that had no relationship with her temple, Christian organizations that helped look after children living on their own, city-run projects to help care for the elderly, and much, much more. Yet, even when she provided material support, always there was the deep, unseen aid she offered through this connection we all share.

However, she saw that ultimately, for people to live freely and go forward in the world as a blessing to all around them, they needed to know

벗어나 자유인이 될 수 있는 도리를 가르치는 일이 더 시급함을 느끼셨다. 누구나가 다 가지고 있는 참나, 이 내면의 밝디밝은 진수(眞髓)를 알게 하여, 자신들이 자유롭게 사는 것은 물론이요, 자신들의 삶이 인연 맺은 모든 이에게 축복이 되어 이 한 세상을 활달이 살아갈 수 있도록 해야겠다고 다짐하셨다.

마침내 산에서 내려온 스님께서는 1972년 경기도 안양에 한마음선원을 설립하셨다. 이후 40여 년 동안 한마음선원에 주석하시며, 지혜를 원하는 자에게 지혜를, 배고프고 가난한 자에게는 먹을 것과 물질을, 아파하는 자에게는 치유의 방편을 내어주시는 무한량의 자비를 베푸시며 불법의 진리를 가르쳐 주셨다. 스님은 도움이 필요한 다양한 사회복지 프로그램을 후원하셨고, 6개국에 10개의 해외지원과 국내 15개의 지원을 세우셨다. 또한 스님의 가르침은 영어, 독어, 스페인어, 러시아어, 중국어, 일본어, 불어, 이태리어, 베트남어, 인도네시아어, 아랍어 등으로 번역 출간되었다. 스님은 2012년 5월 21일 자정, 세납 86세로 입적하셨으며, 법랍 63세셨다.

about this bright essence that is within each of us. To help people discover this for themselves, she founded the first *Hanmaum*[5] Seon Center in 1972. For the next forty years she gave wisdom to those who needed wisdom, food and money to those who were poor and hungry, and compassion to those who were hurting.

---

5. Hanmaum[han-ma-um]: "Han" means one, great, and combined, while "maum" means mind, as well as heart, and together they mean everything combined and connected as one. What is called "Hanmaum" is intangible, unseen, and transcends time and space. It has no beginning or end, and is sometimes called our fundamental mind. It also means the mind of all beings and everything in the universe connected and working together as one. In English, we usually translate this as "one mind."

본 저서는 대행큰스님의 법문을
한국어와 영어 합본 시리즈로 출간하는
〈생활 속의 참선 수행〉시리즈 제11권으로써
1991년 5월 5일 정기법회 때 설하신 내용을
재편집한 것입니다.

This Dharma talk was given by
Daehaeng Kun Sunim on Sunday, May 5, 1991. This is
Volume 11 in the ongoing series,
Practice in Daily Life.

Daehaeng Kun Sunim founded ten overseas branches of Hanmaum Seon Center, and her teachings have been translated into twelve different languages to date: English, German, Russian, Chinese, French, Spanish, Indonesian, Italian, Japanese, Vietnamese, Estonian, and Arabic, in addition to the original Korean. For more information about these or the overseas centers, please see the back of this book.

진짜 통하게 되면

1991년 5월 5일

　형제 법우님들, 앞으로는 우리 공부하는 사람들이 점점 늘어나야 합니다. 더욱더 마음[2]을 계발해서 천체를 앉아서 조절할 수 있는 그런 능력을 우리 모두 스스로 배출시킬 수 있어야 하고 또, 다른 분들도 그렇게 할 수 있도록 도와야 합니다. 이건 정말이지 절실한 일입니다.
　이런 걸 여러분이 아실는지 모르겠습니다. 부처님 법은 무조건입니다, 무조건! 여기에 대해 조그만 예를 하나 말씀 드리겠습니다.

---

2. 마음: 단순히 두뇌를 통한 정신활동이나 지성을 일컫는 말이 아니라, 만물만생이 지니고 있으며, 일체만법을 움직이게 하는 천지의 근본을 뜻함. '안에 있다, 밖에 있다' 혹은, '이거다 저거다'라고 말할 수 없으며 시작과 끝이 없고 사라질 수도 파괴될 수도 없음. 시공을 초월하여 존재함.

Inherent Connections:
Children, Parents, and the Dharma all around us

May 5, 1991

Going forward, we all have to develop this practice of relying upon our fundamental *mind* [6] to the extent that we can take care of whatever confronts us, including even problems of a global scale. We also need to share this practice with others and help them to develop their own inherent ability so that they can use it for themselves. This is something most serious and urgent.

I'm not sure if you're aware of it, but this inherent nature of ours, which is also the fundamental nature of reality, functions without hindrance or limitation. Truly!

---

6. Mind(心)(Kor. –maum)**:** In Mahayana Buddhism, "mind" refers to this fundamental mind, and almost never means the brain or intellect. It is intangible, beyond space and time, and has no beginning or end. It is the source of everything, and everyone is endowed with it.

예전에 여기 나이 드신 처사님 한 분이 계셨는데 그분이 패혈증으로 사흘을 못 넘긴다고 의사 셋이 다 그랬습니다. 그런 걸 "몸에 꽂은 거 다 빼고 죽든지 살든지 나갑시다." 하니까 말도 못 하고 고개만 끄덕거리더군요. 그때 무슨 생각을 했느냐 하면, 이유는 불문에 붙이고 무조건 이 사람은 누구든지 데려갈 수가 없다고 그랬습니다. 무조건이요. 왜 그랬느냐? 예전에 상원사(上院寺)를 지을 때 여러 가지 상황이 급박했을 때에도 그랬었지만 그런 상황에서는 무조건이지 이유가 붙어서는 안 되기 때문입니다. 무슨, 어려워서 못살겠네, 죽겠네, 이것이 잘못됐네, 저것이 잘됐네 이런 게 붙으면 그건 진짜 부처님 법이 아닙니다.

Let me give you one, very small example of this: There was an old man who practiced in this temple, and happened to come down with acute blood poisoning. Several doctors all confirmed that he had only a few days to live. I went to his hospital room, and seeing him there, I said, "Let's get rid of all those tubes and needles, and live or die, get out of here." He couldn't speak, but nodded his head weakly. At that moment, because the situation was so desperate, I raised the thought that, no matter what, this man would not be carried off. No matter what!

This fundamental nature functions without hindrance or limitations, so we too need to raise thoughts free of fear, attachments, and limitations! Yet, if we get hung up in ideas such as, "It's too hard," "I can't take anymore," "That's no good," and so on, how can we function as our true nature, working in accord with this great, unhindered reality?

In the early 1960s, when I was helping to rebuild Sangwon Temple (in the Chiak Mountains), I encountered all kinds of difficult situations. To overcome those, I couldn't dwell on reasons or excuses; I just had to approach the situation unconditionally.

부처님 법이란, 묘하고 슬기롭고 진짜 아무것도 붙지 않는 그 자리에서, 눈은 샛별같이 떠지고 한생각[3]이 불끈 (주먹을 쥐어 보이시면서) 솟을 때의 그 무조건적인 생각! 이런 생각이 모두를 건질 수 있는 겁니다.

그거는 크고 작고가 없습니다. '나는 이렇게, 이렇게 꼭 하겠노라!' 하고 주먹을 불끈 쥘 때, 마음속에서 정말 절절한 눈물을 흘리지마는 눈은 생동생동하게 더 똥그랗게 떠지고 눈에서 불이 번쩍번쩍 나는, 이러한 그 '무조건'의 생각, 그겁니다.

---

3. 한생각: 어떤 생각을 우리들 내면의 근본자리에 입력시키거나 맡겨 놓았을 때, 근본을 통해 나오는 생각은 우리들 몸속의 모든 생명들뿐만 아니라 이 세상의 만물만생에 전달되며, 일체가 그 생각에 응하게 됨. 보이지 않는 정신계, 즉, 우리들 근본마음을 통해 일으켜지는 생각은 물질계에서 현실로 나타나게 됨. 이렇게 근본을 통해 나오게 되는 생각을 한생각이라 함.

If we give rise to a thought from this utterly unhindered, wise, and profound reality that's sometimes given the name "*Buddha-dharma*,"[7] then such a thought functions as one with everything and so can save everything. There is no "big" or "small" in this.

When I make up my mind to do something [she thrusts her fist into the air in a sign of determination], I throw my whole heart into it. Even if the pain coming to me from the situation fills me with tears, I keep my eyes firm and unwavering. We have to raise intentions in this way – fearlessly and free of all discriminations.

If you take *Juingong*,[8] something that is inherently part of you, and set it up as if it were

---

7. Buddha-dharma: In general this refers to the living, breathing, fundamental reality that the teachings of Buddha point towards, but it occasionally means the teachings themselves.

8. Juingong(主人空): Pronounced "ju-in-gong." Juin (主人) means the true doer or the master, and gong (空) means "empty." Thus Juingong is our true nature, our true essence, the master within that is always changing and manifesting, without a fixed form or shape.

Daehaeng Sunim has compared Juingong to the root of the tree. Our bodies and consciousness are like the branches and leaves, but it is the root that is the source of the tree, and it is the root that sustains the visible tree.

주인공(主人空)[4]을 어떤 대상으로 놓고 그냥 구렁이 담 넘어가듯 '주인공이 해 주겠지.'라고 한다면 주인공 따로 있고 여러분 따로 있게 되는 겁니다. 그러면 여러분의 생각이 법이 되질 않아요. 물론 이런 것도 여러분의 지혜 물리가 터져야 알 겁니다. 관(觀)[5]이란 내 주인공이 있다는 것을 내 주인공이 증명하는 겁니다. 또 지금 내가 말한 내 근본에 무조건 맡기라는 것도 관입니다. 어떠한 문제를 꼭 해야만 되겠다 할 때 무조건입니다, 무조건! 거기에는 아무 이유가 붙지 않아야 된다 이 소립니다.

지금 여러 가지 생각이 올라오죠. 그런데 망상은 끊어야 될 그 어떤 것이 아닙니다. 바로 여러분에게 물리가 터지게 할 수 있는 수련 재료이자 여러분을 성장시키는 과정이죠. 그렇기

---

4. 주인공(主人空): 우리 모두 스스로 갖추어 가지고 있는 근본마음으로 일체 만물만생의 근본과 직결된 자리. 나를 존재하게 하고, 나를 움직이게 하며, 내 모든 것을 관장하는 참 주인이므로 주인(主人)이며, 매 순간 쉴 사이 없이 변하고 돌아가 고정된 실체가 없으므로 빌 공(空)자를 써서, 주인공(主人空)이라 함.

5. 관(觀): 어의적으로 '관찰하다' '보다'라는 뜻을 가지고 있으며, 마음공부를 하는 과정에서는 '참나'인 주인공을 믿고 맡기는 것을 뜻함. 즉, 삶에서 부딪치는 모든 문제들을 주인공만이 해결할 수 있다는 철저한 믿음으로 주인공에게 맡겨 놓고 분별없이 집착 없이 지켜보는 것을 통틀어 '관'이라 함.

some kind of deity, praying to it and asking it to take care of this and that, then because you're viewing this part of yourself as something separate, the thoughts you give rise to will have no power to manifest into the world.

Of course, you'll see this for yourself after you awaken. The very act of relying upon your foundation is your Juingong, or "true doer," proving its existence. And, completely entrusting even what I've just said is also relying upon your foundation. When, from deep inside, you feel that something absolutely must be done or resolved, then do it unconditionally. Unconditionally! Just jump straight in!

Similarly, people sometimes get caught up in notions such as cutting off useless thoughts; however, all the different kinds of thoughts that arise aren't just things to be cut off. They are materials for your practice, and the stuff that will make it possible for you to grow up and awaken.

Thus, these "false" or "useless" thoughts aren't something to get rid of – just acknowledge them and move forward. If you're too concerned about these things, then that worry itself becomes a hindrance to you. Those concepts of "false" and

때문에 망상을 끊지 않고 **여여**(如如)[6]하게 그대로 넘어가야 합니다. 망상을 한다고 여러분이 생각을 하니까 망상이죠. 망상이라는 이름도 사람이 지어 놨지 누가 지어 놨겠습니까? 그런 말에 흔들리지 마십시오.

줄창 말하지만, 이 세상에 누구나가 다 수 억겁에 걸쳐서 엄청나게 힘든 과정을 걸어왔습니다. 그랬는데 그것도 모자라서 또 지금 여기에 휩쓸리고 저기에 휩쓸리면서 진짜 부처님의 골수를 놓치고 갈 겁니까? 위 속눈썹하고 아래 속눈썹하고 같이 작용을 하는 정도로 가까운 것이 부처님 법입니다. 부처님은 자기와 아주 가깝게 있으니 멀다고 생각을 하지 마시라 이겁니다.

요새 암이나 백혈병이라고 하면 사람들은 그 이름에 그만 눌려서 포기를 해 버리는 마음이 생깁니다. 뼛속으로 썩어 들어가니 고통스럽고 두려워서 포기합니다. 무엇이든 여러분이 포기를 하니까 포기가 되는 겁니다. 이건 여러분이 절실히 느껴야 합니다.

---

6. 여여(如如): 만물만생이 평등하고 차별 없이, 어디에도 머물지 않고 끊임없이 흘러 돌아가고 있는 그대로의 모습. 일체가 고정됨이 없이 돌아가는 진실의 모습을 말하며, 이러한 진리의 흐름에 부합하는 삶을 살아가는 것을 여여한 삶이라 함.

"delusive" are just things somebody else made up; don't let yourself be disturbed by them.

Everyone in the world has gone through extremely difficult times to get to where we are now. Wasn't that enough? Do you really want to go on like that forever, always suffering and being swept away by this or that, unaware of the very marrow that makes it possible for you to live?

The essence of this is right before your very eyes. It's in everything you do, and is fundamental to every aspect of your ordinary, daily life. This marrow, this Buddha essence is right there with you, so stop thinking it's somewhere far away. This mysterious functioning is always right in front of us, and is so profound.

Look at the world around us. When a doctor says words like "cancer" or "leukemia," just hearing those words often paralyzes people with fear and causes them to lose all hope. As the disease eats into their bones, in their suffering, they panic and give up. Because they give up, they are given up. To put it another way, the lives in their body give up and the surrounding world abandons them as well. The principle behind this applies to everything. You really need to understand this.

언젠가 한 번 이런 예가 있었습니다. 어떤 사람이 골수에 전부 병이 들어서 썩어 들어간다는 겁니다. 그 속에서 벌레가 뼈를 긁어 먹는다고 의사가 그러더랍니다. 병원을 여섯 군데나 다니면서 진찰을 해 봐도 다 그러더라는 겁니다. 내가 그때에 이런 말을 했습니다. "그거는 그렇게 긁어 먹는 병이 아니라, 그냥 우리가 감기 조금 들어 있는 거나 마찬가지야." 그 사람이 이 도리를 알면 좋은데 모르니까, 그 사람에게는 마음을 편안하게 해 주는 게 우선이라 이렇게 말해 줬습니다.

그리고 또, 이건 절대로 그런 병이 돼서는 안 된다고 아주 작심하라고 그랬습니다. 어찌됐건 그 사람은 그렇게 병원에 다니면서 치료비를 대느라 집도 땅도 다 팔아 나중엔 정말이지 남의 행랑채에 살아야 할 정도로 더 이상 어쩔 수 없는 처지가 되었습니다. 그 사람은 이 공부를 모르기 때문에 그 방법밖에는 할 수가 없었어요. 이 부처님 법은 부처님 법 그대로가 약인데 말이죠.

There was a man who heard from the doctors that a disease had spread throughout his bone marrow. They told him that bacteria were eating away the inside of his bones. He received the same diagnosis from six different hospitals. He came to see me, so I looked carefully at him and told him that his bones were actually free of anything serious. Instead, it was just something similar to a cold.

It would have been nice if he had understood this principle, but he didn't know anything about it. So, the first thing I had to do was get him to let go of his fears and put his mind at ease. To begin with, I told him to give rise to the very firm determination that he would never have that disease.

In order to pay for medical treatments and hospital visits, he had already sold his house and lands. By the time he came to see me, he was living in a tiny room at someone else's house. He didn't know anything about this practice, so I had to give him something to hang on to. Ultimately, it's not the particular medicine that cures people: it's the functioning of the Buddhadharma that enables that medicine to help people.

그래서 그 사람에게 이렇게 얘기했죠. "감자 살 돈은 좀 있느냐?" 그러니까 그 돈은 있대요. 그럼 감자를 사서 즙을 내 거기에 미숫가루를 멀겋게 타서 간식으로 먹으라고 그랬습니다. 또 맛있게 해 먹으려면 누런 설탕 사다가 가미해서 그냥 먹으라고 그랬습니다. 그런데 여러분 한 번 생각해 보세요. 그게 그 병을 낫게 할 수 있는 겁니까? 그게 거기에 맞는 처방이 되는 겁니까? 하지만 그 사람은 진짜로 그렇게 하면 자신이 살 수 있다고 믿었습니다. 의학적 지식이 있는 사람 같으면 그거 안 믿었겠죠. 자식들이 칠 형제나 되고, 쉰 살에 늦게 아들을 낳았는데 병까지 얻었으니 마음이 얼마나 힘들고 아팠겠습니까? 상황이 어려워서 그랬는지 감사하게도 그 사람은 그걸 진짜로 믿었고 그로 인해 쉰 살에, 늦게 낳은 막내아들 덕을 보면서 지금까지도 살아 계십니다. 어떻게 이런 일이 가능했을까요? 그래서 아리송한 게 이 부처님 법입니다. 아주 정말이지 이것은 알다가도 모를 일입니다.

This wondrous Buddha-dharma itself is truly the medicine.

So next, I asked him if he had enough money to buy a small bag of potatoes, and he said that he did. I told him to grate the potatoes and squeeze the juice out of the pulp using a piece of cheesecloth. After letting it settle, he should drink the clear liquid between meals, with some roasted grain powder mixed in. If the taste was too strong, he could add a little brown sugar to sweeten it.

Think about this: does potato juice sound like it should work for such a disease? Yet he had deep faith in what I said, that he would be fine. If he'd had a lot of medical knowledge, he probably wouldn't have had any faith in what I said.

He had seven children, the last born when he was fifty, so you can imagine how desperate his circumstances were once he became ill. Yet thanks to his faith, he is alive today, and is looked after by the son who was born when he was fifty. All of this is possible because of the mysterious and profound nature of the Buddha-dharma. Even after you think you understand it, it continues to surprise you.

나는 가끔 패혈증에 걸렸던 그 처사님한테 한 것처럼, 이유는 불문에 붙이고 "무조건 안돼!"라고 할 때가 있습니다. 보이는 세계에 나오는 모든 거는 보이지 않는 세계로부터 나온 거거든요. 그래서 딱 진(陣)을 쳐 놓고선 "안 돼! 절대로 안 돼!" 하면 아예 그냥 못을 콱 (주먹을 불끈 쥐어 보이시면서) 쳐 놓는 거나 다름없는 겁니다. 그렇게 더러더러 했습니다. 왜냐하면 내 가슴이 너무 아파서요. 사람이 죽고 살고, 또는 믿고 안 믿고 그걸 다 떠나서 말입니다. 그럴 때 그렇게 내는 그 마음은 정말이지 굵은 **불바퀴**[7]를 그냥 콱 (주먹을 쥐어 내리쳐 보이시면서) 박는 것과 같아, 아마 이 세상이 다 없어진대도 그건 빼지 못할 겁니다.

여러분이 이렇게 마음 냈을 때 돌아가는 이치를 참다웁게 아신다면 정말 여러분이 법신(法身)[8]이요, 불부처요, 산 부처요, 화신(化身)입니다.

---

7. 불바퀴: 만물만생이 지니고 있는 영원한 생명의 근본(불성)이 서로 직결되어 있어서 시공을 초월하여 끝없이 함께 돌아가며 작용하는 것을 뜻함. 에너지를 발산하는 수레바퀴에 비유하여 불바퀴라 표현함.

8. 법신(法身): 부처의 마음이 중생들을 구제하기 위하여 여러 모습으로 나타난다고 하는데, 보신(報身), 응신(應身)(혹은 화신(化身))과 함께 삼신(三身) 중의 하나. 진리를 체득한 깨달음의 본질이 현실에서 작용하게 되는 것으로, 대행큰스님은 근본자리에서 올라오는 마음이 발현되는 것이 법신이라고도 설명하심.

Sometimes, when I encounter a critical situation or someone in great need, a great determination arises within me – "No! Absolutely not!" Everything in this visible world begins in the unseen realms. Raising up a firm and absolute "No! Never!" is like driving a nail into the problem in the unseen realms, so that it can't manifest. [Holding up a clenched fist.] I do this because I feel heartbroken when I see people suffering; it doesn't matter who they are or what they believe. Raising this kind of firm intention takes the energy of the universe and nails the problem in place, so that it can't move in a harmful direction.

If you are able to truly know how things work, then when you raise intentions in this way, you will naturally be fulfilling the role of a Buddha and manifesting the Dharma. Here, there are no words such as "sufficient" or "lacking," "right" or "wrong," "rich" or "poor," "noble" or "lowly." Words, labels, and theories have no place here.

To reach this point, you have to gather together all of your sincerity and keep gathering it into your foundation again and again, as if

여기에는 글자도 붙지 않고, 이론도 붙지 않고, 더한다 덜한다, 이게 옳다 그르다도 붙지 않으며, 가난하다거나 부자라는 것도 붙지 않고, 위대하다 위대하지 않다도 붙지 않습니다. 진실한, 그 뼈저린, 아주 진한, 바닷물을 다 모아서 한 방울이 되는 그 피 한 방울이 말해줍니다. 이건 말로 형용할 수가 없는 겁니다. 난 어저께도 그저께도 그그저께도 너무 가슴이 아파서, 눈물이 한없이 쏟아지려는데 누구한테 보일 수 없어서 속울음을 울었지만 눈이 생둥생둥하게 떠지면서 기둥이 와짝 (주먹을 쥐어 보이시면서) 섰습니다.

한 가지 더 얘기할 게 있습니다. 우리는 지금 정신계로 치닫고 있습니다. 공부하시는 여러분이 한생각을 내서 둥글려서 모든 걸 해나가신다면 우리 나라는 진짜 융성하게 될 겁니다. 그런데 조그만 그릇에다가 재료를 많이 넣어서 막 흘러내리지 않도록 하세요. 되레 부작용이나 가지고 야단들을 하지 않도록 우리는 제대로 해야 됩니다. 그런데 시간과 약속은 하지 마세요. 그럼으로써 자라나는 새싹들이 나중에 주인이 돼서 살 때, 그 밑으로 밑으로 내내 선맥(禪脈)이 끊어지지 않고 끝간 데 없이 이어질 수 있게 할 수 있는 법신들이 필요한 것입니다.

you were trying to squeeze blood from your own bones. When this ocean of sincerity has been gathered together into a single drop, well, words just can't describe that. Something came up recently that left me so heartbroken that I've wanted to cry for the last three days; but from this ocean, a single harmonious thought arose like an iron pillar and became one with the whole. As that great energy began to burst forth, my eyes became bright and strong.

We are coming to a time when it will be desperately important that you all know how to work through the unseen realms. If practitioners can raise thoughts from their foundation and take care of things harmoniously and non-dualistically, then this world of ours will survive and truly flourish.

Of course, as you practice, you should be careful not to overstep your ability; otherwise, your efforts can end up causing all kinds of negative effects and chaotic situations. If a small bowl tries to hold too much, its contents will overflow and cause countless problems. Similarly, don't try to force timetables onto your practice or attainment.

그래서 마음공부[9]에 대해 이야기를 하면 어떤 사람들은 왜 학술적으로 하지 않고, 경전으로 하지 않고 그렇게 딴말을 하느냐고 합니다. 풀 한 포기에도 생명이 있고 이심전심으로 말을 전달하고, 같이 공생(共生)을 하고 공식(共食)하고 있는데 무엇이 부처님 법이고 무엇이 부처님 법이 아니겠습니까? 진리가 그러하기 때문에 가톨릭교인이고 기독교인이고 모두 다 너무나 공감하고 좋아하는 겁니다.

지난 번에 샌프란시스코의 한 호텔에서 설법을 한다고 기별을 하니 정치적으로나 종교적으로 보수적인 사람들뿐만 아니라 다양한 종교의 지도자들도 왔습니다. 설법이 끝나고 그 중의 몇몇 분들과 저녁식사를 함께 했는데 그분들이 그러더군요. 어떤 질문을 해도 당신은 어떻게 그렇게 서슴지 않고 대답을 해 줄 수 있느냐고, 그러면서도 남에게 해롭게 대답도 하지 않고, 어떤 거 하나 나쁘다는 것도 없이 그렇게 대답을 할 수 있느냐고 말입니다.

---

9. 마음공부: 진정한 자유인이 되기 위해 자신의 마음이 어떻게 작용하고 변하는지를 관찰하고 배우며, 그것을 실제 생활 속에서 응용하고 체험해 보면서 알아가는 모든 과정을 뜻함.

We need true practitioners who can go forward practicing through mind in this way, which is the true tradition of Seon, and who can help raise the future generations of practitioners that the world is going to need.

Sometimes people complain that I don't quote the sutras or teach from them when talking about spiritual practice and our fundamental mind. But what is there in this world that is not part of Buddha's teachings? Even a single blade of grass has life and communicates mind to mind with everything else, sharing the same life and freely giving and receiving whatever is needed. Everything is just truth itself, so even people of other religions can appreciate what I say.

The last time I was in San Francisco, I gave a Dharma talk at a hotel. A lot of people came, including politicians, conservative religious figures, and leaders from other religions. Afterward, a number of us had dinner together, and during the conversations several of them were amazed that I could answer so many questions without any hesitation. They were likewise impressed at how harmonious my answers were, and how anyone could benefit from them, regardless of their beliefs.

내가 지금 이런 말을 하는 것은 내가 잘났다는 얘기를 하는 게 아니라 부처님 법이 그렇다는 겁니다. 내가 잘났다고 해 봐야 이 고깃덩어리가 얼마나 잘났겠습니까? 부처님이 말씀하신 가르침의 골수는, 여러분들이 **오신통(五神通)**[10]을 벗어나야 불바퀴를 굴릴 수 있고, 다시 그 불바퀴도 벗어나야 여러분들의 마음이 천백억화신으로 화해서, 바깥으로 전 우주 삼천대천세계(三千大千世界)를 들락거리면서 용도대로 이렇게 저렇게 쓸 수 있다는 겁니다.

여기서 지구를 한번 살펴보죠. 인간이라고 하는 개체 안에 마음, 생명이 있기 때문에 모든 것들이 우리네들 온 몸을 통해서 나고 들고 하는 것처럼, 지구도 살아 있는 생명들이 모여 있는 물질이자 행성이라 많은 입자들이 여러 경로를 통해 들고 나고 있습니다.

---

10. 오신통(五神通): 불교의 육신통(六神通) 중에서 누진통(漏盡通)을 뺀 다섯 가지의 신통(능력), 즉 천안통(天眼通), 천이통(天耳通), 타심통(他心通), 숙명통(宿命通), 신족통(神足通)을 일컬음. 천안통(天眼通)은 보는 사이 없이 볼 수 있는 능력, 천이통(天耳通)은 듣는 사이 없이 들을 수 있는 능력, 타심통(他心通)은 다른 이의 마음을 아는 사이 없이 알 수 있는 능력, 숙명통(宿命通)은 과거 어디로부터 왔는지를 아는 사이 없이 아는 능력, 신족통(神足通)은 한 찰나에 가고 옴이 없이 가고 올 수 있는 능력을 말함.

This is the nature of the truth the Buddha spoke about, which is why I bring this experience up, not because I want to boast about something. The profound and sincere essence of the Buddha's teachings is such that when you have attained the *five subtle powers*[9] but are free from attachments to them, you can then freely share and apply this energy that connects everything. When you can step beyond even this stage, then, through mind, you can manifest in ten million different ways, freely coming and going throughout all realms, and naturally taking care of things as needed.

Let's take a look at the Earth. It, too, functions like this: it's a material, functioning system where living beings are gathered together, and where particles are continuously coming in and going out through many different routes.

That which we call the *Dharma realm*[10] connects everything both on and beyond the

---

9. Five subtle powers(五神通): These are the power to know past and future lives, the power to know others' thoughts and emotions, the power to see anything, the power to hear anything, and the power to go anywhere.

10. Dharma realm(法界): The level of reality where everything functions as an interpenetrated and connected whole. Daehaeng Kun Sunim said that this can also be called the Dharma Net, and compared it to our circulatory system, which connects and nourishes every single cell in the body.

그리고 이러한 지구 안에 펼쳐져 있는 세계를 위해 지구 안팎과 연계되어 돌아가는 법계가 있는데 거기엔 커다란 세 가지 소임이 있습니다. 아주 질서정연하게 단계 단계 돌아가고 있지요. 안으로 들이고 바깥으로 내는 소임, 안으로 바깥으로 전부 통신하는 소임, 그리고 책정을 하는 소임, 이렇게 세 가지를 가지고 있습니다.

그 중에 안으로 들이고 밖으로 내는 소임에 대해 얘기할 때 그걸 넓게 보자면, 우리가 지금 땅에 발을 붙이고 다니는 것도, 남극과 북극에서 들이고 내는 그 소임을 하기 때문입니다. 남극이 똥 누는 데라면 북극은 먹어야 하는 곳입니다. 우리 인간이 필요한 건 먹고 나머지는 배출하면서 살듯이 지구도 그러하다 이겁니다.

Earth. It also performs three major functions that support life on the Earth: it controls what leaves and what enters the Earth; it controls communications both on the Earth and outside of it; and it determines what is necessary and responds accordingly. All three of these functions work together smoothly and harmoniously.

For example, it's the Dharma realm's role of controlling what enters and leaves that makes it possible for the North and South Poles to function. This, in turn, is what makes it possible for us to move by stepping on the Earth. The Earth functions just like humans: when we eat, we absorb what we need and excrete the rest. Likewise, if the North Pole is where energy enters, then the South Pole is where what's left leaves.

In the case of human beings, this same fundamental essence manifests as unseen particles from our mind itself – you could say that it's the manifestation of our Buddha essence working to protect humans in five different ways. Without this protection and the abilities it makes possible, it would be impossible for us to even walk. It's one of these abilities that makes it possible for

그런데 인간의 경우에는 우리네들 마음 자체의 보이지 않는 입자, 즉 말하자면 화신들이, 그렇게 세 가지로 아니, 다섯 가지로 나뉘어져 보호하고 있습니다. 만약에 그렇게 보호하지 않는다면 우리는 걸어 다닐 수가 없습니다. 그 중 하나는 우리가 무언가를 끌어 잡아 당긴다거나 끌려가게 하는 양면을 잘 잡아서 책정을 하는 작업입니다.

세균이 들어와도 우리가 들여 놓을 건 들이고 내놓을 건 내놔야만 하는 작업이 있죠. 지금 이 허공에도, 내 몸 안에도 세균이 그냥 욱시글득시글하니까요. 또 인연에 따라서 유전성으로 어떤 문제들이 생긴다거나 영계성으로 무언가가 침입을 한다면 우리는 살기가 무척 힘들어집니다. 예를 들어, 임신을 했을 때 제대로 조정을 못하고 아무거나 다 받아들이면 태아에 이런 것들이 마구 들어와 그 애가 이 세상에서 대통령을 할 만한데도 소통령도 못하게 만들어 놓을 수도 있는 거죠. 이런 식으로 가다 보면 우린 미래세계에서 정신세계의 노예로서 살게 될 겁니다. 우린 뜻한 바대로 살 수가 없어요. 내일 어떻게 될는지 모레 어떻게 될는지도 몰라요.

us, from the place of our Buddha essence, to appropriately regulate what we draw toward us and what pulls on us. For example, even the air around us is filled with microbes, and while some are good for us, there are others that should be kept out, or sent out.

Microbes aren't the only thing that we have the ability to regulate, nor are they the only thing that we must regulate. If in the course of our unfolding *karmic affinity*,[11] genetic problems were to arise, or ghosts were to enter a person, those could make someone's life very difficult indeed. For example, if you are pregnant and those sorts of things are allowed to enter without any control or filtering, then they could enter the fetus and cause serious problems. A child who may have previously had the potential to be president of a country may now not be able to lead even small groups.

If humans try to live without learning to apply this Buddha essence, we will end up as slaves to the unseen realms. Should this come to

---

11. Karmic affinity(因緣): The connection or attraction between people or things, due to previous karmic relationships.

부처님께선 "네가 네 정신을 가지고 있고, 네가 네 주인공을 가지고 있으니, 안으로도 노예가 되지 말고 바깥으로도 노예가 되지 말라."고 하셨습니다. 그 말씀은 자기 주장자[11]가 있다면 이렇게 저렇게 끌려 다니진 않을 것이지만, 자기 주장자가 없어 집이 비었다면 수없는 게 들락거리면서 그 집을 망가뜨린다는 뜻입니다.

네 주인이 있어 네 집이 빈 집이 아니라면 내 주인을 너에게 보내 한마음[12]으로 하나가 돼 가지고 일을 크게 할 텐데, 네 주인, 즉 주장자가 없으면 내 주장자를 너에게 한데 합쳐 줄 수 없죠.

---

11. 주장자(柱杖子): 일반적으로 선사(禪師, 스님)들이 좌선할 때나 설법할 때 들고 다니는 지팡이를 말함. 행을 통해 흔들리지 않는 마음의 중심이 서게 되는 것을 뜻함. 마음공부 과정에서는 안팎에서 일어나는 모든 문제를 내면의 근본마음 한 곳에 맡겨 놓는, 참선수행을 통해 흔들리지 않는 마음의 중심이 서게 되는 것을 말함.

12. 한마음: '한'이란 광대무변함, 일체가 하나로 합쳐진 것을 뜻하며, 한마음이란 만질 수도 없고 보이지도 않으며, 시공간을 초월하여, 시작도 끝도 없는 근본마음을 말함. 또한, 만물만생의 마음이 삼천대천세계와 서로 연결되어 하나로 돌아가는 것을 의미하기도 함. 다시 말해, 한마음은 우주 전체와 그 속에서 살고 있는 일체 생명들이 근본을 통해 서로 연결되어 그 마음들이 하나로 돌아가는 모든 작용을 포함하고 있음.

pass, we would have no control over our lives, with each new day bringing only chaos. This is why the Buddha said words to the effect that you already have your foundation and self-awareness, so learn to live freely and be a slave to neither the material realm nor the unseen realms. There's no time to waste. None of us knows what will happen tomorrow.

Which is to say, live firmly centered on your foundation. Then, you can't be dragged this way or that. However, if you aren't centered upon your foundation, you're like an empty house that has no owner – countless beings are able to wander in freely and will end up destroying your house.

When you are fully present as the owner of your own house, I can send my energy and ability to you, and they can become one with yours and do great works. However, if you aren't there in your house, your body, then I can't send anything to you. If there's no owner, your body is like an empty house, and all kinds of beings, including human spirits and animal consciousnesses, can freely enter and leave. Coming and going as they wish, they create all sorts of problems and end up destroying your body. With a broken down

자기 주장자가 없다면 자기 몸은 빈집이 돼서 털구멍, 눈구멍, 콧구멍을 통해서, 보이지 않는 데서, 온갖 사람들의 영혼뿐만 아니라 짐승들의 의식도 드나들기 때문에 몸이 망가집니다. 그렇게 몸이 망가지면 자기에 대해 생각해 볼 수 있는 마음공부를 못 하게 되고, 내가 나를 찾는 것도 여간 어려운 일이 아니게 될 겁니다.

그래서 몸을 망가뜨리지 않기 위해 석가모니 부처님께서는 몸으로 고행을 하지 말고 정신 수행을 하라 하신 거죠. 일체를 들이고 내는 것을 진짜로 누가 하고 있는지 그 참나를 알라고요. 몸은 사대로 흩어지고 말지만 너의 참마음은 끝간 데 없이 너를 살리고 너의 중생을 살리고 수많은 외부의 중생들을 다 건질 수 있다고 하셨습니다. 그리고 또 석가모니 부처님께서는 "위로 억만 분이 깨달으셨다 하더라도 한 도량에 한 부처니라. 그러니 평발 한 발로 디뎠느니라."고 하셨습니다.

and crumbling body, it's hard to even think about spiritual practice, let alone to actually meet your true nature.

The Buddha, too, told people not to follow ascetic practices that just end up destroying the body. Instead, he taught that we should practice through mind. He wanted us to know that which is really doing all things. He also said that although our body returns to its basic elements, this true mind of ours endlessly saves us; it saves the lives that make up our body, as well as countless beings outside our body.

Sakyamuni taught that even though millions of beings awaken, they are all still just one Buddha, right here. The great feet of Buddha have already reached every corner of the universe. In other words, even though millions of beings have awakened, your true mind is right here, functioning as one with everything, and it's this true mind that can save you, as well as the land you live in. And when you can transcend time and space and become one with the awakened ones, the fragrance of your true mind will spread throughout the world and function in all manner of ways. Isn't this a wonderful teaching?

이 말은 억만 분의 깨달으신 분이 있다 하더라도 지금 이 도량을 구하는 건 그 분들의 마음과 하나가 된 네 참마음이며 이렇듯 시공간을 초월해 하나가 된다면 그 마음이 이 세상에 두루 작용할 거라는 뜻입니다. 그러니 얼마나 갸륵한 말씀이냐는 거죠. 『금강경』이나 『화엄경』이나 『반야심경』을 보면 그 말을 그렇게까지 구체적으로 안 하셨어도 거기에 글자 아닌 글자로 아주 탁탁 박아 넣었죠.

엊그저께 어느 스님이 "왜 『반야심경』을 한문 그대로 하지 않고 한글로 풀이해서 하느냐?" 그러더라구요. 그건 예전에 부처님께서 하신 좋은 말씀을 한문으로 적어놓은 게 있으니까 지금도 그걸 그대로 해야 한다고 말씀하시는 거잖아요? 그렇다면 예를 한 가지 들어 보겠습니다.

그 시절에 물건을 옮길 때, 지게꾼을 불렀다면 지금은 트럭을 불러야 됩니다. 트럭을 불러야 하는 지금 "지게꾼! 지게꾼!" 하고 부르면 트럭 운전수는 자기가 아니라 지게꾼을 부르니까 대답도 안 합니다. 그런데 지금 "지게꾼! 지게꾼!" 하고 부르란 말입니까? 내가 이렇게 말을 했더니 그 스님이 싱긋이 웃으면서 "그러네요. 스님 말씀이 옳습니다. 참, 우리가 못 하는 걸 당신이 해 줘서

The Buddha taught this same idea in the *Diamond Sutra*, the *Flower Garland Sutra*, and the *Heart Sutra*. Even though the idea wasn't expressed this explicitly, it's still there, written very clearly in words that are not words.

A few days ago, a visiting Buddhist monk said to me, "The *Heart Sutra*, just as it is, has an incredibly profound power to it. Why is your temple using a modern, Hangeul translation instead of the traditional version?" What he meant was that the Buddha's teachings, as written down so long ago, should be chanted without any modifications.

So, I gave him the example of what we used to call an "A-frame porter." These were the guys who used an A-frame pack to carry and deliver stuff. When someone needed help moving something they would send for a porter, but nowadays people use a truck or a moving service.

If you were to go around shouting for a "porter," nobody would respond, would they? Because they're not "porters," they're "movers" or "moving companies." When I said this, the monk laughed, and said he was grateful there was someone who had the ability to truly translate the sutras.

얼마나 감사하고 좋은지 모릅니다. 그런데 스님이 이렇게 잘 되시니 배가 아프기도 하지만 부럽기도 합니다."라고 하시더군요. 허허허…. (대중 웃음)

오늘은 설법하는 날이 아닌데 하다 보니까 이런 말이 나왔습니다. 그런데 내가 잘하니까 나를 믿고 따르라는 게 아니라, 본래 부처님이 가르쳐 주신 이 진리가, 뜻이, 법이, 중용이 바로 그러하다는 겁니다. 이제 모두 질문들 하십시오.

질문자 1(남): 제가 질문 드리려고 했던 것에 대해 큰스님께서 지금 법문을 하시면서 대부분 다 말씀해 주셨습니다. 자비로우면서도 크나큰 법문을 듣고 당황하고 흥분해서 어찌할 바를 모르겠습니다.

오늘은 습(習)[13]에 대해서 여쭙겠습니다. 사람의 마음이 원래 찰나찰나 돌아가기 때문에 습이 붙을 자리도, 업(業)이 붙을 자리도 없다고 말씀하셨습니다. 그럼에도 불구하고 우리 중생은

---

13. 습(習): 현재뿐만 아니라 과거 수 억겁 년 동안 행하였던 모든 행위들(말, 행동, 생각 등)이 버릇이 되어 잠재여력으로 남아 있는 것을 말함.

I've been talking about a lot of different things today, but don't misunderstand my intention. I'm not trying to awe you or imply that you should follow me. Rather, I mean that the truth, the middle path that the Buddha taught, is so profound and great. If you would follow anything, follow that.

Now, let's see if there are any questions.

Questioner 1(male): I'd like to ask you about *habits*.[12] In the past, you've said that our mind is constantly changing and flowing, so fundamentally there's no place for habits to stick to, nor is there even any place for karma to attach. Yet even though this is so, somehow, for eons, unenlightened beings have created habits and then been caught up in those habits, going through untold suffering because of them.

---

12. Habits(習): These include not just the ways of thought and behavior learned in this life, but also all of those tendencies of thought and behavior that have accumulated over endless eons.

몇 억겁을 거치면서 습이 쌓이고 쌓여 가지고 그 습에서 벗어나지 못하고 고통 속에서 살아가고 있습니다. 그런데 체가 없는 마음에 이렇게 습이 붙어 이생에 와서 중생들이 고통 속에서 살아가고 있는데 어떻게 해야 될지 잘 모르겠습니다.

큰스님: 아, 그 얘기하는데 뭐가 그렇게 깁니까? 첫째, 무조건 '네가 있다는 것을 네가 증명하는 거다.' 하고 관하고, 둘째, '가정살이 돌아가는 것 전부를 그놈이 하는 거다.' 하고 관하는 거예요. 그놈이 모든 것을 다 하는 건데 뭐가 그렇게 답답하고 힘듭니까? 나는 잘되고 못되는 것을 떠나서 말하는 겁니다. 어떤 답답한 것도, 잘 안되는 것도, 잘되는 것도 거기서 나오는 겁니다. 그렇지만 이것을 그냥 알기만 하는 데 그쳐서는 안 됩니다.

아까 내가 얘기했죠. 모든 것이 다 내 근본에서 나오는 거라고요. 내일 죽는다, 지금 죽는다, 우리 식구가 다 멸망한다 이러더라도

Having carried around these habits that are causing us so much pain for so long, how can we ever be free from them?

Kun Sunim: It's fairly straightforward. First, you need to entrust everything that arises back to your foundation, along with the very firm thought, "Okay, true self, you need to prove that you exist!"

Second, deeply trust your inherent foundation, and know that it has the power to truly take care of what's going on in your life and family. So entrust all of that stuff there, and let it work! It's your true nature that's doing everything, so why do you need to feel so choked and burdened? Leave behind all ideas about whether things went well or not. Whether something is frustrating, going badly, or going well, it's all being done by that essence.

But you can't stop at the point where you only know this fact. As I said earlier, absolutely everything arises from your foundation. So, if you can entrust everything to your foundation, if you go straight in, if you are fierce in your determination to let go of attachments to "I," even

눈 하나 깜짝하지 않는, 결사적인, 나를 버린 그 마음으로 정통으로 들어간다면 뭐가 그렇게 어렵습니까? 뭐가 답답합니까? 진짜 우주간 법계와 삼천대천세계의 모든 일체제불이 우리와 한 골수에 들어서 한자리를 할 수 있는데 말이죠.

그렇게 어렵고 답답하게 느끼는 것은 다 욕심 때문입니다. 그렇게 생각 안 드십니까? 욕심을 부리지 않고도 그냥 닥치는 대로 늠름하게 넘어갈 수 있는데 말이에요. 칼을 빼야 될 때는 그냥 쏙 빼면 됩니다. 그 때 악한 마음으로 칼을 뺐을 때는 당연히 사람을 죽이는 칼이 되고, 살리기 위해 칼을 뺐을 때는 수많은 중생들을 다 살릴 수 있고, 한 나라를 세울 수 있는 겁니다. 그런데 뭐가 그렇게 답답합니까?

내일 죽으면 어떻고, 지금 죽으면 어떻고, 식구가 다 죽으면 어떻습니까? 아니, 이 말이 너무 잔인하고 심하다고 생각하십니까? 아휴! 우리는 이 세상을 그냥 살 뿐이에요. 이 길을 그냥 걸을 뿐이에요.

in the face of fears about your own death or your family members, then nothing else will bother you or be that difficult. Why do you need to feel so suffocated when all the Buddhas in the universe can become one with you? It's your greed and desire that makes you feel like that.

Even though you don't give rise to ambitions, you can still overcome everything you encounter with your head held high. If you have to use a sword, then pull it from its sheath without hesitation and hold it high. Of course, if you draw your sword with an evil mind, then it can kill people; but if you draw it forth to save people, then it can save countless people and even build a country.

There's no need for things to be so difficult. What's the big deal if we die today instead of tomorrow, or if even our whole family dies? Does what I am saying seem too severe? [Sighs.] We're just passing through this world. We just walk forward in life doing our best with what confronts us. Still, you need to realize why you're here and what you have to do with your life. When you understand this, it will be like a great weight has been lifted from you.

그런데 내가 어디서부터 이렇게 와서 지금 무엇을 하고 가는지 알아야 답답하지 않다 이 소립니다. '야! 이거 뭐 캠핑 와서 잠시 있는데 내가 이렇게 생각하고 행동하는 것이 다 그 우주간 법계에 통신이 되는구나. 이럴지언대 내가 뭘 그렇게 걱정하랴.' 이렇게 생각한다면 하나도 걱정할 게 없어요. 이 세상이 다 없어진대도 걱정할 것이 없습니다. 내 마음이 그 정도가 돼야 세상을 살릴 수가 있는 거지, 하나하나를 다 걱정하는 사람이 어떻게 세상을 건지고 살릴 수 있습니까? 가정문제도 마찬가지입니다. 이판사판이에요. (대중 웃음) 죽느냐 사느냐 이거뿐이지 거기에 또 뭐가 붙습니까?

예전에 어떤 스님이 날더러 이렇게 말하더군요. "스님, 제가 이 토굴에 들어가면 문에 못 좀 박아 주십시오." 그래서 "못은 왜?" 하고 물으니 "들어간 뒤에 바깥에서 못을 박으면, 죽지 않으면 얻을 거 아닙니까? 죽지 않으면 얻고, 얻지 못하면 죽고 이거 둘뿐 아닙니까?"라는 겁니다.

View your stay in this world like just a brief camping trip, thinking, "Even though I'm out here, the Dharma realm knows everything I feel and experience. It's always looking after me, so what do I have to worry about?" If you go forward with this attitude, then truly, you won't have much to worry about. Even if the entire world were about to be destroyed, you wouldn't be worried about anything. When your mind is this settled, you can actually save the world.

But how could you do this if every little thing rattles and worries you? All of this is true for family problems as well. Frankly, there aren't really any alternatives: we have to either become someone like this, or we will be swept away.

Once there was a sunim who only half-jokingly asked me to nail shut the door of the tiny hut he was staying at. He said he would go in, and then I would nail the door shut behind him. I asked him why he wanted me to do this; he answered that if he couldn't leave the hut, there would be only two choices: awaken or die.

If you understand the principle I was just talking about, you can go through life with a relaxed, generous heart. As you go forward one

여러분이 이 도리를 알면, 아주 너그럽게 살아갈 수 있고 너그럽게 두루할 수 있고, 남이 반 미쳤다고 할 정도로 항상 싱그레 웃으며 길을 걸어갈 수 있어요. 죽으러 가는 소 무리를 봐도 싱그레 웃을 수 있어요. 그 소들이 죽으러 가는데도 가엾다는 생각조차 없습니다. 왜냐하면, 바로 그 순간에 곧바로 마음으로 들어가서 건지기 때문입니다.

소 만 마리가 모두 죽었다고 하더라도 그렇게 마음으로 건지면 그것은 마치 빗방울 하나 하나가 모여 큰 바다로 흘러들어 가게 하는 것과 같죠. 그리고 그렇게 바다와 합쳐지면 한 그릇이지 그게 두 그릇입니까? 우리의 마음은 근본을 통해 하나로 돌아가니 일심(一心)이자, 그 능력이 무궁무진하니 무량심(無量心)이에요. 묘법(妙法)이죠. 그런데 그 많은 소들이 죽으러 가는 걸 보고 불쌍해서 염불을 해 주고 그런다면 그건 이 마음도리를 잘 모르는 사람이에요. 지금 그 소들이 죽으러 가는데 무슨 염불이 필요합니까? 염불하다 보면 벌써 늦는데요.

with all, you breathe life into everything you encounter, and smile so much that people think you're nuts.

Even if you see a bunch of cows on their way to the slaughterhouse, you can smile without any fears for them. You don't have any pity at all for them because, through mind, you can immediately become one with the cows' minds and save them instantly. Even though ten thousand cows died, if you can save them like this, then it's as if you're gathering individual raindrops and helping them flow to the sea. And when those raindrops meet the sea, they are all just one. There is only the water of the ocean. This is so marvelous.

Our minds function as one through the foundation, so this is called "one mind." The ability of this one mind is so powerful that sometimes it's called "Immeasurably Vast Mind," and sometimes it's just called "the Profound Dharma." If there's someone who feels pity for cows on the way to the slaughterhouse but who then tries to help them by going and chanting at the temple, well, I can only say that they don't understand this principle. You need to be able to save them all right now. If someone understood

그러니까 이 마음도리를 알고 진정으로 깨닫는다면 그 순간에 생명들을 구할 수 있다는 얘깁니다. 만 마리고 천 마리고 모조리 이 한 그릇, 자기 마음에다 넣으면 그냥 다 자기 한 그릇이 되니까요. 자기가 돼 버리는 거죠. 그렇게 근본을 통해 자기와 하나로 만들어 놓는다면 그 생명들은 인간으로 진화되어 나갈 수 있는 거예요. 그리고 그 한 그릇 속을 거쳐서 나가는 인간은 인간이 돼도 그냥 아무렇게나 사는 그런 인간이 되는 게 아닙니다. 정말 사람 노릇을 하고 이 세상을 두루 살필 수 있는 지략과 아량과 지혜가 충분한 사람이 되는 겁니다. 그런데 뭘 어떻게 살아야 될지 모르겠다고 하는 겁니까? 뭐가 답답하다는 겁니까? 그렇게 답답한 마음으로 살면 자손도 잘 될 수가 없어요. 장관 할 정도의 그릇이라면 그 정도는 하고 가야 할 것 아니에요.

질문자 1: 큰스님 앞에서 이렇게 법문을 들을 때는 금방 제가 부처가 될 것만 같고 하늘을 날 것 같습니다.

this principle of one mind, they wouldn't wait until later.

So, if you truly awaken and understand this principle, then you save beings in the same instant that you become aware of their need. Whether it's ten cows or ten thousand, when you entrust them all to your foundation, they become one with you. One mind. And becoming one with you like this helps them a great deal in evolving into human beings.

Furthermore, those who have evolved through one mind, when they are finally born as humans, will be people of high quality. Such people would be great beings – resourceful, full of tolerance and wisdom, and able to help take care of the world. We all have this potential, so don't allow yourself to live a narrow, miserable life. If you're always caught up in small things, the influence of that will also make it hard for your children to live up to their potential.

Questioner 1: When I hear your teachings like this, I feel like I'm about to awaken and fly into the sky like a bird.

큰스님: 이것 보세요! 부처가 되려고 하지도 말아요. (대중 웃음) 이 세상에서 부처가 되려고 하는 마음이 있다면 답답한 마음이 또 생길 테니까요. 그러니까 순서를 밟으며 못났든 잘났든 그대로 그냥 수순히 걸어가세요. 입 딱 다물고 그냥 마음 딱 세우고, 그냥 걸어가다가 무슨 일이 닥칠 때는 "네가 하는 거지." "너!" 하면 그건 그냥 그대로 깜짝할 사이죠.

물론 그 마음작용이 체(體)로 만들어져 나올 때는 시간이 걸리겠지만, 그렇게 한번 마음을 내면 바로 자동적으로 불이 확 붙어서 끓는 쇠가 되니 뭐든지 거기다 다 집어 넣으면 나올 수 있는 건 바로바로 나오게 돼 있어요. 그런데 그렇게 약한 마음으로 이 도리를 어떻게 공부하겠어요?

누구나 이 세상에 잠시 왔다 가는 겁니다. 그러니 지금 가난하니까 부자가 되기 위해, 지금 병고가 있으니 병 없이 살려고, 위대하게 되려고 이 공부 하지 말아요, 진짜로요! 그런 것 때문에 이 공부 하지 마세요. 어려움이 닥쳤을 때 단호하게 그냥 "안 돼! 이거는 내가 안 된다면 안 되는 거지!" 하란 말이에요. 나도 그랬어요. 말도 안 되는 어려움이 닥칠 때마다 "안 돼!" 하면서 그냥

Kun Sunim: Look! Don't try to awaken! [Laughs.] If you're focused on something called "awakening," you'll wind up filled with frustration.

Take yourself as you are, and in each stage of your practice, just keep going forward on the path in front of you, taking things as they come. Be focused, calm, and centered on your foundation. And when something serious hits you, hit back with, "Hey! Let's take care of this!" From that instant on, it will begin to change.

Of course, it usually takes some time for the results to work their way into the material realm. But as you entrust things in this way, then, like a blast furnace heating up, there will be cases where your foundation instantly melts down what you've entrusted, and immediately sends it back into the world with a new shape. But how could someone experience this if they aren't relentless about entrusting the situations and emotions that confront them?

Everyone is just passing through this world for a short time – just visiting and then leaving – so don't waste your energy chasing riches, fame, or even health. And don't use this practice

왁 소리를 지르곤 손을 번쩍 쳐들어서 내쳤단 말이에요. 그 마음이 진짜 깊은 물이 되기 때문에 큰 배가 뜰 수 있고, 큰 배가 뜰 수 있기 때문에 거기 중생들을 다 태울 수 있는 겁니다.

그러니까 첫째 일요일에는 우리가 항상 서로 토론하고 공부를 해 나가면서 그 쓰리고 아픈 상처를 아물게 하고, 내 몸에 들어 있는 모든 중생들을 제도할 수 있도록 합시다. 그러면 그 제도된 중생들이 천백억화신으로 들락거리면서 나와 남을 위해서 일하고, 나라를 위해서 일하고 전 세계를 융화시킬 수 있겠지요.

그리고 전 세계를 융화시키고 건지려면 우리가 집도 잘 지켜야 합니다. 지구라고 하는 우리의 집을 잘 지켜야 하는 것도 우리의 소임이고 내 몸이란 집을 잘 지켜야 하는 것도 소임입니다.

to chase after those. When you do encounter something very serious or dangerous, firmly raise the thought, "No! It should go like this!" This method really works. When I realized that incredibly serious situations were developing, I would shout "No!" and slam my fist on the table. A mind like this becomes deep waters, thus large boats can sail there and take many beings across.

Thus, for the sake of our practice, let's always try to leave time for discussion and questions when we have these first Sunday Dharma talks. And through our practice, let's heal our wounds and lead all the beings within us to enlightenment. Then those awakened beings within us will constantly leave our body and return, functioning as a billion manifestations of Buddha nature as they work for the well-being of yourself, others, society, and for the harmony of the world.

In order to be able to bring harmony to the world and save others, we have to take care of our house, the Earth. Taking care of this house called the Earth is one of our duties, and taking care of the home that is our body is another of our duties. You've received your bones and flesh from your

여러분이 부모에게 뼈를 받고 살을 받았는데 그 몸을 건강하게 잘 간직해서 살아 있는 동안 수행을 잘 하고 갈 수 있도록 해야 합니다. 인간이 돼 가지고 진짜 사람이 못 된다면 어떻게 효를 다했다고 할 수 있겠습니까? 부모에게 잘해 드리고 잘 입혀 드린다고 효가 아닙니다. 진짜 인간이 됨으로써 부모에게 효도를 다하는 거다 이겁니다.

오늘이 어린이 날이라면서요? 그런데 나는 그것도 모르고 아까 "오늘 애들 오면 뭘 좀 줘야지."라고 했더니 스님들이 "오늘이 어린이 날이라서 다 준비해 뒀어요."라고 하더군요. 그래서 너희들이 나보다 천배 만배 낫다고 했어요.

그거는 그렇고 효도에 대해 좀 더 얘기하죠. 어느 부모든지 자식이 아프고 어디가 병들었다고 한다면 부모 마음이 얼마나 아픈지, 그거는 자식들 입장에선 상상조차도 못할 겁니다. 나가서 다녀도 좋은 게 없고 아무리 우스운 일이 있어도 웃음이 나오지 않는 그런 부모가 돼 버리고 맙니다.

parents, so it's your duty to take good care of those and do your best to become a true human being.

Even though you're born with a human body, if you aren't trying to become a true person, how could you say that you've honored your parents? Being a good son or daughter doesn't mean just being respectful and taking care of your parents. Leading a good life and becoming a true person is the way to truly repay your parents.

I didn't realize that today was Children's Day until just before the talk. I said to the sunims here that we should prepare some snacks or something, because a lot of kids would undoubtedly come with their parents today. But the sunims were a step ahead of me, and had already prepared all kinds of Children's Day treats. They're so wonderful!

Okay, let's talk a little more about what it means to be a good daughter or son. When children are sick or hurt, parents feel terrible, don't they? Nothing's fun anymore, and laughter disappears from your life. No one truly realizes what parents go through until they themselves become a parent.

그러니까 몸을 함부로 다루지 말아요. 젊은이들이 젊은 혈기에 자기 몸을 마음대로 막 굴리면, 그건 효도도 못 할 뿐만 아니라 충성도 못 하죠.

또, 상구보리(上求菩提) 하화중생(下化衆生)[14]이라고 그랬잖아요! 몸이 망가지면 그 안에 들어 있는 자기 중생을 제도 못하니 자기 집이 더 망가지는 거고 결국은 자기 집 속에서 사는 자기의 의식들도, 인연들도 다 그냥 끊어지는 거예요. 그럼 우리가 보내고 있는 지금 이 시간을 어떻게 보내야 될까요?

우리가 과거, 현재, 미래를 나눠서 많이 얘기들 하죠. 앞으로 올 시간을 갖고 말할 때 미래라고 하고요. 그런데 정신세계에서는 과거도 현재도 미래도 다 한자리에 있으면서 불바퀴처럼 돌아가는 거예요. 원래는 이처럼 공해서 돌아가니까 여러분이 죽고 사는 생사의 문제에 끄달리지 않는다면 지금 이 자리가 바로 본래 그 자리요 오늘이 바로 영원한 그 날입니다.

---

14. 상구보리 하화중생(上求菩提 下化衆生): 위로 깨달음을 구하고 아래로 중생을 교화한다는 뜻. 위로는 진리를 깨치고 도를 이루어 부처가 되려고 정진하는 동시에 아래로는 고해에서 헤매는 일체중생을 교화하려고 노력하는 것을 말함.

So don't be stupid with your body. When young people are overflowing with energy and do things that damage their body, it often becomes hard for them to be of help to their parents or their country.

There is a well-known Buddhist teaching that says we should practice and attain enlightenment, and save all those lost in ignorance. But, when your body is breaking down and being destroyed, it's so very hard to even practice, let alone awaken and be able to save the beings within your body. Further, if you can't help those beings, then this house of yours will fall into disrepair even faster. If you can't help them evolve, then they can't help you evolve, and if this continues, it becomes a vicious cycle where any evolution is very, very difficult.

Then how do we need to spend our time? People think that there are things like the past, present, and future, don't they? Yet in reality, the past, present, and future are all one, and functioning as the energy that connects everything. They are all inherently functioning and flowing like this, so if you are not caught by life and death, and are free from attachments and

얼마 전에 사무장님이 나보고 사월초파일 메시지를 써달라고 그러더군요. 4월 8일은 아직도 멀었는데 왜 벌써 쓰라고 하느냐고 했더니 지원에 미리 돌려야 되니 일찍 써야 한다고 그러는 거예요. 그 소리를 듣고 받아 쓰라고 불러줘 놓고는 자기가 해 놓은지를 모르는 거예요. 그리고 좀 있다가 사무장님더러 읽어 보시라고 그랬죠. 그런데 누가 썼는지 잘 썼더라고요. 그래서 "그거 누가 했는지 3단계로 곧잘 했구나." 그랬어요.

정신세계는 그런 거예요. 미래에 있을 일에 대해 처리하면 이미 했으니 과거가 되어 놓고 가는 거고, 그리고 그게 지금 벌어지고 있으니 현재인 거죠. 석가모니 부처님이 태어나셔서 우리가 그 뜻을 기리는 초파일도 마찬가지입니다.

fears about those, then you can live in accord with this eternal moment where the past, present, and future are all one.

A couple of weeks ago, our office manager asked me for the short, one page Dharma talk that will be read out during the Buddha's Birthday celebrations. I was a bit surprised, because Buddha's Birthday was still a month away. But he said that they needed it early in order to send it out to all of our overseas branches. This made sense, so I told him to write down what I was about to say, then I spoke. I just spoke from deep inside, without really being aware of what I was saying.

After he finished writing, I asked him to read it back to me. As I listened, I saw that the talk nicely explained the functioning of the truth in three stages. That Dharma talk was something I was doing for the future, which I was taking care of in the present, and as soon as I spoke, those words were in the past. I'd already let go of it and moved with the present moment. The past, present, and future are a flowing whole like this, so every instant is the moment Buddha appeared in the world.

그 뜻은 여러분이 있는 이 장소에서 지금 그대로 존재하고 있습니다. 4월은 바로 동서남북 전체를 말하고 8일은 유(有)·무(無), 말하자면 사무사유(四無四有)를 가리킵니다. 즉, 안 보이는 세계와 보이는 세계가 한데 합쳐져서 시공을 초월해 돌아간다는 뜻을 나타내는 것이 바로 초파일입니다. 이 얼마나 좋은 의미를 가지고 있는 날입니까? 이렇듯 부처님이 태어나신 장소가 따로 없고 시간도 따로 없기에, 영원한 부처님 오신 날일세 한 겁니다. 그러니 여러분들은 그 뜻을 깊이 깊이 생각하시어 영원한 오늘임을 새겨야 합니다.

이 못난이 말이 맞죠? 어떻게 생각하세요? 허허허. 사실 여러분도 못났고 나도 못났고 부처님도 전부 못났어요. 그리 못났으면서도 부처님께서는 진리를 깨닫고 나서는 가섭에게 **다자탑(多子塔)**[15] 앞에서 당신 자리의 반을 탁 내주면서 앉았단 말입니다. 야, 참! 그것은 이

---

15. 다자탑(多子塔): 부처님께서 중인도의 다자탑에서 설법하실 때 가섭존자가 누더기를 걸치고 뒤늦게 나타났는데 여러 제자가 못마땅하게 여겼지만 부처님께서 앉았던 자리의 반을 내 주면서 같이 앉자고 하셨음. 한마음에서 모두가 둘이 아니라는 뜻을 가르치고 두 자리가 아니라는 뜻을 가르친 것임.

This means that the Buddha exists right here, where you are now. You can see this even in the date of the Buddha's birthday. It's April 8th, right? [On the Korean lunar calendar] April is the fourth month, and the number "4" means East, West, South, and North, i.e., every direction, every piece. When we add another "4" to this to include all of the "directions" of the unseen realms, then "8" symbolizes everything throughout all visible and invisible realms. So April 8th means everything throughout all realms working together and transcending time and space.

Isn't this a wonderful meaning? It means that the Buddha is here in this very moment. He never left, nor did he come from somewhere else. This very moment where you are is the eternal moment of the Buddha appearing in the world. Please engrave this deeply within your heart.

So what do you think now about the meaning of the Buddha's Birthday? Although imperfect, I did a pretty good job with this, didn't I! [Laughs.] In truth, I am imperfect, you are imperfect, and the Buddha is imperfect. Even though he was imperfect, he still awakened to the truth, and later in front of the assembly of monks, he

세상에 조금도 버릴 것이 없는 한자리였습니다, 한자리. 이 이야기를 가르치기 위해서 반 자리를 내주신 그 뜻이 얼마나 깊습니까? 그런데 우리는 이 이야기를 읽어 보기만 하지 그 뜻을 새겨 보지를 않아요. 아마 이런 이야기들에 대해서는 세상 사람들이 나보다 잘 알지도 몰라요. 그리고 불자라면 더 많이 알겠지요. 그런데 그 이야기들의 깊은 속을 모르고 또 행하기가 그렇게 어렵다 이겁니다. 또 질문하실 분 있으시면 질문하십시오. 오늘은 시간 제한하지 말고 우리 그냥 푹 빠져보죠. 하하하….

질문자 2(남): 큰스님께서 저희들을 공부시키면서 몰락 놓으라는 말씀을 자주 하시고, 때로는 무조건 맡기라고도 하십니다. 그런데 맡기는 놈은 누구이며 맡는 놈은 또 누구인가 하는 의문이 떠오릅니다. 결국은 맡기는 자와 맡는 자가 모두 나 자신이라는 걸 느끼게 되었습니다.

moved over and asked *Kassapa*[13] to sit beside him. How wonderful! He was showing us that we are all inherently one, that we all share the same supreme, perfect place.

In order to teach people this wonderful, supreme meaning, he shared his seat with Kassapa. Unfortunately, people often just glance at these kinds of stories without deeply reflecting on them. They've heard many similar stories, but it's not easy to understand the deep meaning those stories carry, nor to put that meaning into action.

Does anyone have any further questions? Please ask if you do, and let's not worry about the talk running long today.

Questioner 2(male): When you teach us, you often say to let go of everything unconditionally and entrust it to our foundation. Yet I found myself wondering who is doing the letting go

---

13. Kassapa, or Maha Kassapa: Regarded as the foremost of the ten great disciples of the Buddha. He was well known for his self discipline, and the Buddha himself praised Kassapa for his attainment and realization. After the Buddha's passing, Kassapa was chosen to lead the great council that gathered to record the teachings of the Buddha.

또, 놓고 맡기는 거기에 아무런 경계가 없다는 생각도 듭니다. 그렇다면 놓는 것도 맡기는 것도 없는 셈이 되는데, 큰스님께서는 '놓아라 놓아라' 하시니 이게 어떻게 된 노릇인지 궁금합니다.

큰스님: 지난번에도 내가 얘기했죠. 큰 솥에다 팥죽을 쑤는데, 팥죽 방울이 수도 없이 그냥 막 끓어오른단 말입니다. 여러분 뱃속에서도 수없는 생명의 의식들이 나옵니다. 요 방울 조 방울, 요 방울 조 방울이 연방 나오는데, 한 가지로 고정되게만 나온다면 무슨 걱정이겠습니까마는 천차만별로 다른 방울이 그냥 솟아 나와요. 그런데 그 천차만별로 다른 방울이 바로 한 죽솥에서 나오는 거니까 거기에다 다 놔라 이런 겁니다. 나오는 데도 한군데, 놓는 데도 한군데다 이거예요. 예전에 어느 스님이 죽을 쑤면서 '조놈도 문수! 요놈도 문수!' 하고 죽방울이 나오는 대로 주걱으로 쳤다지 않습니까?

and who is receiving, and I have come to the conclusion that both are myself. It seems like I'm doing both, so there should be no need to let go, because everything is already right here, but you still teach us to let go. What am I missing?

Kun Sunim: When you make red bean porridge, you have to boil it, so thick bubbles continually arise. Big bubbles, small ones, single ones, and groups of bubbles all come out one after another, just like the thoughts and emotions that continuously arise within us. Anyway, bubbles of all kinds arise within that porridge, yet all of those arise from the porridge and are porridge, so just let them return back to the porridge.

What I'm saying is return it all to the place it comes from. If the bubbles in the porridge were all one size and always arose in the middle of the pot, they wouldn't be a big deal. But sometimes they arise at the edges, and sometimes they're huge, so if they burst on their own, before the cook pokes them, they spray hot porridge everywhere and cause problems. Thus, the story of the sunim who was cooking porridge: as bubbles formed, she

우리가 살림하다 보면 별의별 걱정이 다 생깁니다. 아파서 걱정, 돈 없어서 걱정, 회사에 가서 상사들한테 꾸중을 들어서 걱정, 애들이 속을 썩여서 걱정, 또 부부지간에 싸워서 걱정, 뭐, 걱정이 한두 가지가 아니죠. 그러니까 '죽방울은 죽방울인데 그렇게 다른 죽방울이다. 그런데 그것들이 다 한 죽솥에서 나온다는 것을 알아라. 그러니 나온 데서 다 해결할 거라고 믿고 거기에 몽창 놓는 거다.' 이렇게 되는 거예요.

어떤 것이 나오더라도 그 자리에서 나왔으니 걱정을 하지 말고 그 자리에 그냥 맡기세요. 당장 애가 나가서 죽는다며 난리를 치더라도 걱정을 하지 마시고 '모든 건 거기에서 나온다.'라는 거를 알고 그 자리에 모든 걸 맡기신다면 그 애는 그런 행동을 하지 않습니다. 왜냐하면 내가 생각한 것이 벌써 전체 통신이 되기 때문이죠.

would poke them with a spoon, saying, "You are *Manjushri*,[14] and you, and you, too!"

In the course of our day-to-day life, all kinds of concerns and worries arise. We find ourselves worrying about our health, money, problems at work, being criticized by our boss, our kids behaving badly, fights with our husband or wife, and just every kind of thing. Yet all of those are just bubbles in the porridge. They are porridge, and they all arise within the same pot, so return them all back to this place they're arising from. Have faith that the place they arose from is also the very place that can resolve them.

No matter what kind of situations or feelings arise, they still come from your foundation, so just return them there and don't let yourself fall into worries. Even if your child storms out, saying they're going to kill themselves, don't give in to worry. Remind yourself, "Even this arises from my foundation," and entrust it all there. If you

---

14. Manjushri: The Bodhisattva who represents the essence of wisdom. Manjushri is traditionally portrayed holding the sword of wisdom in his right hand, and in his left hand holds a blue lotus that represents the flowering of wisdom, while riding a lion that represents courage and majesty. In temples and paintings, he is often together with Samantabhadra.

통신이 되는 것은 통신망이 이미 가설이 되어 있기 때문입니다. 저 사람이 내 형이라는 거, 내 아들이라는 거, 내 마누라라는 거, 내 엄마라는 것을 알잖아요.

여러분들한테 이미 가설된 가족이라는 단단한 통신망이 있습니다. 그러니까 급하면 급한 대로, 가까운 사이면 가까운 대로, 마음내면 내는 대로 다 알아요. 그러니 내가 한생각을 그렇게 하는 동시에 바로 식구들까지도 다 통화가 돼요. 거짓말 아니에요. 통신이 된단 말입니다. 그러니 애가 집을 나갔다 할지라도 '난 집으로 들어가고 싶다.' 이러곤 집에 들어오죠. 이런 마음의 통신은 자동적이에요.

이렇게 이심전심으로 마음이 통해 작용해야 자동적으로 두 마음이 아니고 한 마음으로 돌아간다 이겁니다. 그래야 내 마음처럼 상대방이 움직여 주죠.

애들이 잘못하는 것뿐만 아니라 "난 이것을 하고 싶습니다." 하고 다른 의견을 낸다면 어른이 생각할 때 그게 천부당만부당할지라도 "그래, 네가 하고 싶은 거니까 한번 해 봐." 그러고선 아주 좋게 받아 주고 그것이 어떤 것인지만 경험하고 딱 돌아서게끔 마음에다 꽂아 놓으세요.

can do this, your child won't behave in a harmful manner.

Why is this? We are all inherently connected, so when you entrust a thought to your foundation, it is automatically communicated to everyone and everything. It's communicated to the whole, but is often felt the strongest by those closest to us: our brothers, sisters, parents and children.

For example, when you feel that something is urgent, or feel affectionate, they can sense that. So when you entrust a thought to your foundation, in that instant, it's communicated to your family. It really happens like this. The thoughts you raise really are communicated to them.

So if your child runs away, raise warm, caring thoughts for them, and sooner or later, your child will want to come back home. The thoughts you entrust are sent to them automatically. You don't exist apart from each other; both of you are together within one mind. How could they not respond to your concerns?

Suppose your child really wants to do something that, to you as an adult, seems totally unreasonable. You should still be open to it, saying, "Okay, if you really want to do that, go

그러면 부모와 자식 간에 통신망이 가설이 돼 있기 때문에 아이가 나가서 하고 싶은 것을 다 해 보고, 아니다 싶으면 "아이, 아버지, 나 그거 그만두겠어요." 하고 자연스럽게 얘기 합니다. 그리고 그 말을 들은 아버지는 오히려 "왜 그만두니?" "괜찮아, 네 생각대로 해." 그러거든요. 그러면은 아이는 "아, 이만저만해서 그러니까 저 다른 거 해보겠어요." 한단 말입니다. 이렇게 이심전심으로 사랑과 자비, 의리를 가지고 가정을 이끌어 나가야지요. 이게, 부모의 참 사랑입니다.

그런데 그냥, 애가 나가서 조금만 잘못했다 하면 아이의 이야기는 듣지도 않고 "이놈의 새끼야, 너 하라는 공부는 안하고 어디 갔다가 이제 들어왔어? 이 애비는 땀 흘리며 힘들게 돈 벌어다가 너희들 공부시키는데." 이럽니다. 누가 아니래나요? 하하하…. (대중 웃음)

"그렇게 공부시키는데 요놈 새끼, 뭐 어디 가서 자고 들어와?" 하면서 아이 사정은 알아보지도 않는 겁니다. 속에서 나오는 대로 그냥 막 화를 내버리는 거예요.

ahead. I'll support you." At the same time, you should firmly entrust the thought that it turns into a useful experience for them and others, but that having experienced it, the child will soon lose interest in it.

Then, because this communications network exists between you two, after your child tries that thing, they'll find it wasn't as interesting as they supposed. "Dad, I want to quit that now." "Oh, why?" "You know, it's just okay." And often they'll find something else that interests them more. This is the way to raise your family – communicating directly, through mind, with love, generosity, and trust. This is truly loving someone.

However, when children screw up, parents often just start with the yelling, "Where the hell did you go last night? You were supposed to be studying! Do you know how hard your father works to support you?!" As if kids never notice things like that! [Audience laughs.]

Instead of just leaping to assumptions and making accusations, "You couldn't call?!" "How could you…?!" it would be better to actually listen to the child's explanation. After listening to what

이런 경우에는 내가 먼저 내 얘기를 하기 이전에 상대방 얘기부터 듣고, 잘못됐으면 "애, 이렇게 이렇게 하는 게 좋지 않겠니?" 하고 그 마음이 나온 그 자리에 다시 맡겨야죠.

또, 아이의 얘기를 들어보고 잘못되지 않았으면 "아, 그런 일이 있어서 못 들어왔구나. 그건 잘했다. 네 친구를 위해서 그렇게 했다면 참 잘했다. 사나이가 그런 의리도 없이 어떻게 살아나가겠느냐." 하고 부모가 이렇게 좀 북돋아주면 아이는 나가서 잘못하라고 해도 안 해요.

아이 교육은 부모가 가르치는 일이 삼분의 일이고, 아이가 자기 마음을 스스로 다잡아서 나가는 것이 삼분의 일입니다. 나머지 삼분의 일은 학교에서 선생님이 가르치는 것이죠.

이렇게 교육의 3단계가 잘 이루어지면, 아이는 부모에게 함부로 말하지도 않습니다. "아버지!"라고 부르며 좋아하고, 어려운 일을 말할 땐 바른자세로 정중하게 말하고, 또 웃기고 재밌는 얘기를 할 때도 이랬어 저랬어 하며 마구 말하지 않습니다. 아주 존경하고 어려워하면서도 사랑하기 때문이죠.

your child has to say, if it turns out they really did screw up, then try to suggest something positive that they can do if they find themselves in a similar situation. "Honey, in that case, what about trying...?" while entrusting that situation to your foundation.

If, on the other hand, it turns out that your child had a good reason, then encourage them. For example, if their friend had some family emergency, "Actually, I think that was a great thing to do. What kind of place would this world be if we didn't take care of each other?" With positive encouragement like this, it's very unlikely that children will lose their way or fall into dark paths.

A child's education actually consists of three parts. The first is what they learn from their parents. The second part is what they learn from their teachers at school. And the third part is what they themselves learn from trying to manage their own thoughts and behavior as they go forward in the world.

When all three parts are going well, children are generally respectful and civil towards their parents. When they have to bring up a difficult

지금은 시대 흐름이 빨라져서 예전의 서른 살이 지금 스물 한, 두 살 정도와 맞먹는 것 같아요. 시대가 그만큼 변했으니 아버지, 어머니들은 자녀 교육에 대해 좀 더 생각을 깊이 해 보셔야 될 겁니다.

또 아이를 키울 때는 작은 일에도 신경을 많이 쓰셔야 됩니다. 예를 들어 아이들이 집에 오기전에 외출해야할 경우가 있죠? 그럴 땐 그냥 나가지 말고 부모가 아이에게 관심을 기울이고 있다는 것을 아이들이 알 수 있도록 반드시 몇 자 써서 놓으세요.

"애, 아무개야! 냉장고에 반찬을 넣어 놨으니 그걸 데워서 먹어라. 그리고 언제 들어오는지는 몰라도 좀 일찍 들어와서 배고프지 않도록 해라. 너무 피곤하면 안 되지 않니?" 이렇게 아주 간단하게 써서 상에 놓아두고 나가세요. 그러면 자식들이 그걸 볼 때 차마 그 마음을 나 몰라라 할 수가 없습니다.

subject, they're polite about it, and when talking about something funny or interesting, they don't use foul or rough language. And in general they tend to enjoy talking with their parents, because they respect, esteem, and love them.

The world is moving so fast these days that kids who are only twenty years old are as mature as thirty-year olds used to be. Society is changing this quickly, so parents need to think that much more deeply about how to raise their children.

When raising children, you have to pay attention to all kinds of small things, don't you? If you can't be there when your child returns home, leave some kind words to let them know you care about them. "Honey, I made you some dinner and left it in the fridge. Go ahead and warm it up. I don't know when you'll be coming home, but I hope you don't get too tired or hungry. I love you!" Be caring and centered, but don't let yourself fall into anxiety.

Try to leave your children short messages like this. When they see these, they can't help but be aware of your love and concern, even if they give no outward sign of having noticed it. Kids who grow up in this kind of warmth and love will

그런 사랑과 자비를 받고 자란 아이들은 나중에라도 존경하는 자기 부모를 저버리는 일을 할 수가 없습니다. 이건 절대적입니다. 그게 뭐가 그렇게 어렵습니까? 오늘 내가 이런 말 하는 것은 지금 외국이나 한국이나 자식을 잘 기르는 것이 너무 힘들기 때문입니다. 외국 가면 자녀들이 마약중독 뭐 이런 것이 돼 가지고요, 부모들이 상당히 고생합니다. 또 질문하실 분 있으시면 하십시오.

질문자 3(여): (대중을 향하여) 저는 한국에 안 살기 때문에 오늘이 아니면 여기 와서 스님께 여쭐 수가 없어요. 여러분께서도 스님께 여쭙고 싶은 말이 있으시겠지만 이렇게 제가 질문을 드릴 수 있는 자리를 마련해 주셔서 감사합니다.

저는 20년 전에 서독에 간호원으로 가서 지금까지 일하고 있어요. 다시 서독으로 떠나기 전에 스님께 여쭙고 싶은 것이 하나 있습니다.

저는 아버지가 돌아가시고 어머니 한 분밖에 안 계십니다. 다가오는 5월 8일, 어버이날에 딸자식 된 도리로 어머니께 효도를 하고 싶은 마음도 있지만, 한편으론 어머니에 대한 미운 마음이 그동안 너무 많았던 것 같습니다.

naturally feel close to their parents, even in their old age. This is exactly how it happens.

The reason I bring this up is because whether you live in Korea or some other country, raising kids isn't easy these days. Society has become so complex. Moreover, in some places parents have to worry a lot about drugs, don't they?

Are there any more questions?

Questioner 3(female): I went to Germany in 1971, and have worked there as a nurse ever since. I'm returning in a few days, but would like to ask you about something. My father has passed away, but my mother is still alive. This coming Wednesday is Parents' Day, and while I would like to be a good daughter, I have so much hatred towards my mother.

I had to leave for Germany when I was 25. Even before that, for the first twenty years of my life I suffered so much, I can't even describe it. Even though I excelled in school, I couldn't go to college. Unlike others, I didn't even want to go to Germany, but had to because our family was so poor and needed the money. And for similar reasons, I also never had a chance to marry.

태어나서 20살이 되기까지 피눈물 나게 고생만 하고 남들처럼 제대로 배우지 못했습니다. 서독에도 남들처럼 가고 싶어서 간 것이 아니라 형편이 어려워서 갔어요. 시집을 못 간 것도 서독에 갔기 때문이라고 어머니를 탓하고 원망했어요. 지금은 더 이상 어머니를 사랑하는 마음도 없고 미워하는 마음도 없는 것 같습니다. 그리고 너무 고생하며 살아서 그런지 남들은 괴로우면 울고 기쁘면 웃는데 저는 그러질 못해요. 어떻게 설명해야 될지 모르겠군요. 서독에서 20년간 한국 사람을 상대 안 하고 살아서 대화하기가 조금 힘들어요. 어떻게 하면 제가 이 마음 병을 고칠 수 있을지 스님한테 좋은 말씀을 듣고 싶습니다.

큰스님: 예, 좋아요. 그런데 댁의 고생이 하다못해 천하없어도 나만은 못했을 거예요. 하지만 난 부모에게 너무 고맙고 감사해요. 당신은 예전에 어머니를 미워하다가 지금은 미워하는 마음도 이뻐하는 마음도 없다고 했지요? 그런데요, 댁이 이 세상에 나오지 않았더라면 뭐가 있었겠어요? 미움도 고움도 없었을거고 서독에도 갈 수가 없었을 거예요. 당신이 그래도 어머니를

For years I had so much anger and resentment towards my mother about all of this. Now, though, I just don't feel anything towards her. I have no love for her. She's nothing to me. I guess it's because I suffered so much, but I just can't laugh or cry about things the way normal people do. I'm not quite sure how to explain this; I've lived in Germany for so long, it's hard to fully express myself in Korean.

Kun Sunim, how can I heal this illness of my mind?

Kun Sunim: I understand. While your own hardships may have felt unimaginably severe, my own were actually much worse, believe it or not. Yet I am so grateful and thankful to my parents. You said that you've felt many things towards your mother, such as extreme hatred, and now extreme indifference, right? However, those feelings, and everything else, exist because you appeared in the world and because your mother gave birth to you. Nor could you have gone to Germany, which although difficult, has also given you good things, hasn't it?

빌어서 이 세상에 나왔기 때문에 인생 공부를 할 수 있었고 또 이 공부를 할 수 있었어요. 고생을 했기 때문에 인생 공부를 했지 그게 없었더라면 못 배웠어요. 남이 쓰린지 고운지 또는 아픈지 그거를 느끼지 못했을 거예요. 그런데 그런 거를 느끼게 됐거든요. 곱게 자란 사람보다 더한층 공부를 시켰으니 사자가 사자 새끼를 저 내리막에다가 내팽개친 거와 다름없잖아요?

그러니 고맙게 생각하고 어머니날 꽃을 사서 드리세요. 밉고 이쁘고를 떠나서 무조건 부모에요, 부모란 말이에요. 어머니가 살을 주고, 아버지는 뼈를 줬어요. 당신의 영혼이 거기에 부합이 돼서 삼합이 합쳐져서 당신이라는 사람이 나온 겁니다. 감사히 생각하고 이제는 모든 원망과 미움을 다 버리고 "어머니 감사합니다." 해야지요.

Your mother's existence is what made it possible for you to be born into the world, and because of this, you're able to learn and grow, and also able to learn about your true essence. Because of your suffering you've been able to learn a lot about life and yourself. Without those experiences you would not be nearly as aware of others' pain, love, and resentments. But now you've become a person who can feel deep empathy for others. Your mother indirectly caused you to learn much more than people who grow up in a sheltered environment. In a sense it's like how lions raise their young, by pushing them down hills and river banks so that they learn to claw and fight their way back up.

So just be grateful to your mother, and buy her some nice flowers for Parents' Day. Regardless of how you feel about her, she's still your mother. In Korea, we say that your mother gave you your flesh, and your father gave you your bones, don't we? Your spirit joined with those and became one, and you were born. So be grateful to your parents, throw away all of your resentments, and just say "thank you" to your mother.

이제는 잘못한 거 잘한 거를 무조건 떠나세요. 모든 거를 용광로에다가 집어넣고, 맡겨놓으세요. 그러면 재생이 돼서 다시 이 세상에 나오면 밝게 빛이 날 거예요. 그래야 그 얼굴도 환하게 필 거에요.

꽃을 드리면서 말씀하세요. "이 꽃은 내 마음의 꽃입니다. 어머니 꼭 건강하시고 오래 사세요. 딸 노릇을 꼭 할 겁니다."라고요. 자기 엄마를 가지고 밉지도 곱지도 않다는 게 어딨어요? 아무리 부모가 잘못했더라도 그러지 말아요. 부모는 아마 자식이 아팠던 것보다 몇십 곱절 더 아팠을 거예요. 그거를 알아야지요.

그 때 당시 환경이 그렇게 만든 거예요. 그러면 그 환경을 누가 가져왔어요? 자기가 과거에 그렇게 살았기 때문에 현실에 그 환경이 닥쳐온 거예요. 바로 과거에 자기 산대로 현실에 닥쳐온 거지 누구의 탓도 없어요. 알았어요? 또 이런 일로 마음 아프기 싫잖아요. 그러니 지금이라도 생각을 바꿔요.

It's time for you to walk away from judgments of who did what bad thing. Utterly leave those behind. Drop all of those into the great furnace within you. Turn those thoughts and feeling over to that place; then those things will be melted down and return to the world as something wonderful that can give light to everyone. And your face will shine as well.

Give her the flowers and tell her, "These are the flowers of my gratitude. Please be healthy and live a long time, and I'll try to be a good daughter." You have to let go of your bad feelings towards her. No matter how much she made you suffer, don't give into hatred or resentment. As much as you suffered at the time, your mother was probably going through much worse. Her own suffering was actually many times worse than your own. You need to know this.

It was the extreme poverty of those times that caused both of you to suffer. So, who was responsible for that environment? You both were. How you lived in the past created the conditions that you experienced in this life. So, there's no point in blaming anyone else. You're fed up with suffering like this, right? So now it's time to make a change in your way of thinking.

질문자 3: 네. 감사합니다.

큰스님: (삼배하는 질문자에게) 급할 때는 일배만 하세요.

질문자 4(여): 저도 마음 밝히는 공부를 정말로 하고 싶은데 스님처럼 꼭 출가를 해야만 그렇게 할 수 있는지 여쭙고 싶습니다.

큰스님: 음, 그거는 대답하기가 곤란해요. 그건 자유로 하는 거예요. 하하하….
어쨌든 내가 느낀 거 두 가지를 얘기할게요. 머리 깎고 입산을 한다면 이 공부를 하고자 하는 많은 사람들이 "저 스님한테 가서 공부를 해야겠다." 하고는 와서 배울 수 있어요. 그렇지만 출가(出家)하지 않고도 배우는 거에 있어서는 그냥 스님하고 똑같이 다 할 수 있어요.

Questioner 3: Thank you! I understand.

Kun Sunim: [As the next questioner was bowing three times] When you don't have enough time for three bows, just do one bow.

Questioner 4(female): I really want to sincerely practice and awaken, but I'm wondering if it's necessary for me to leave home and become a *sunim*[15] in order to do so.

Kun Sunim: Hmm. I'm reluctant to say too much because in general this is the kind of thing that people need to decide for themselves, without interference. Off the top of my head though, a couple of things occur to me.

For example, if someone becomes a sunim and practices, then other people who see your gray clothes and shaved head may be inspired to practice themselves, and may come to learn from you.

---

15. Sunim: Sunim is the respectful title for a Buddhist nun or monk in Korea.

무의 세계에서는 출가하지 않고도 다 할 수 있어요. 그런데 유의 세계에서는 이 공부를 잘 모르는 사람들을 더 넓게 가르칠 수가 없으니까 머리를 깎는 거죠.

그러니까 그건 자유에요. 스님이 되고 안 되는 건 자유고, 공부하는 거는 스님이 됐든 안 됐든 똑같아요. 이거는 솔직하게 얘기하는 거예요. 그리고 이 마음 도리도 모르고 스님이 된다면 스님은 돼서 뭘 해요? 아무리 천만 명이 스님이 된대도 껍데기 스님이라면 소용없어요. 그러니까 결심하고 스님이 되는 거, 이거 보통사람들 아니에요. 허허허···.

보통사람들이라면 우리 이렇게 스님 안 돼요. 부모 형제 다 버리고, 모든 걸 다 잘라 버리고, 이 **무명초(無明草)[16]**를 깎아 버리고, '나는 검지도 않고 희지도 않은 도리를 알겠다.'고 다짐하고 들어오는 거, 이거 보통 일 아니에요.

---

16. 무명초(無明草): 불가에서 머리카락을 지칭하는 말로서 번뇌를 상징함. 불교의 출가수행자가 머리를 깎는 것은 무지, 어리석음, 욕심 등에 의해 비롯되는 세속의 번뇌와 얽매임을 잘라내는 결단의 의미를 가짐.

Ultimately, anyone with a sincere mind and determination can study and awaken to the truth. It doesn't matter if they are laypeople or not. Lay practitioners who fully awaken can do anything that's needed in the unseen realms.

However, in the ordinary, visible world, it's hard for them to teach large numbers of people how to practice through this fundamental mind.

It's up to you. You're free to decide to become a sunim or not. Practice doesn't depend upon someone being a sunim or not. I'm being perfectly frank, here. If someone becomes a sunim and never learns about their fundamental mind, then what was the point? Even though a thousand people become sunims, if they don't know anything about this essence, then what does it matter? But a sunim who is determined to know for themselves this truth that encompasses all things is far from an ordinary person. Actually, if someone wanted to live an ordinary life, they wouldn't be thinking like this in the first place. [Laughs.]

Anyway, you could hardly call someone ordinary who leaves their family and everything else behind. To be determined to know and apply

그런데 마음공부를 한다니까 말인데, 어떤 분야에 있든지 이 도리를 배우지 않으면 안 되죠. 만약에 의학공부를 해서 아픈 사람을 건진다 하더라도 마찬가지에요.

학술로 배워도, 이 마음 도리를 체험해서 터득하지 못한다면 마음에서 나오는, 보이지 않는 50%에서 나오는 그 많은 것들을 커버하고 나갈 수 없어요. 그러기 때문에 어떤 공부를 하더라도 의당히 이거는 배우고 나가야 된다는 거예요.

질문자 4: 제가 마음에 걸리는 게 있다면 제가 시집을 안 가고 그냥 스님이 되어서 살 수 있을지, 이게 자신이 없어서 지금 생각해 보는 중이거든요, 스님.

큰스님: 그렇게 생각을 해 보고 있는 중이라면 어떤 방향으로든 단호히 결정을 내릴 수 있는 마음이 들 때까지는 시간이 필요할 거예요. 그런데 시집을 간다 장가를 든다고 하여 모든 정신을 빼앗기는 사람이라면 공부도 못 할 건데 괜히 스님이 돼서 뭘 하겠어요? 가정이라도 잘 지키는 게 좋아요.

this truth that's neither black nor white is certainly not an ordinary thing.

That said, no matter what you do in life or what you study, you still need to understand how this fundamental essence that we all have works. For example, if you work in a medical field, you'll need to know this in order to fully treat your patients. Even if you're a scholar, you'll need to know this as well.

If you haven't experienced and practiced using your fundamental nature – your Buddha essence, your true shape – then you will neither recognize nor be able to take care of the fifty percent of reality that arises from the unseen realms. So, however you choose to live your life, it's proper and natural that you should understand this fundamental nature and be able to work through it.

Questioner 4: My only real concern is whether I can follow the unmarried life of a sunim. This is the part I'm doubting myself about.

Kun Sunim: Well, it sounds like you're better off waiting until it's clear to you what you want

이 공부는 모든 사람을 건질 수 있는 것이고, 앉아서도 이 세상을 다 주름잡을 수 있는 겁니다. 스님이 안 돼도 할 수 있지요.

그럼 뭐가 다르냐? 공부하는 스님네들은 누가 됐든 그 모두와 한마음이 되어줄 준비가 돼 있어요. 한마음이 돼 준단 말이에요. 어떤 상황에서 그게 필요하다고 단호히 결정을 내렸을 때는 우리의 마음이 두 마음이 아니라 전체를 그냥 다 끌어들여서 한마음이 돼요. 한 기둥이 되는 거예요.

그러니까 스님이 되려면 진짜 스님이 돼서 세계를 누비면서 이 마음법을 전파해도 좋겠지요. 우리 생명의 근본이 있음을 알리고, 그리고 모든 걸 체험하고 전해 주는 게 불교니까요.

to do. If someone is constantly pulled back and forth by thoughts of marriage and desire, then it's unlikely they'll be able to fully devote themselves to practice. Then why bother becoming a sunim?

On the other hand, if someone truly understands and applies this practice of relying upon our fundamental mind, they can take care of their family and rescue all beings. They can do this and take care of the entire world, without moving from where they are now. All of this is done through mind, regardless of whether someone is a sunim or not.

This is what true sunims do. They work at becoming one with whomever they encounter. They become one with them. When sunims realize that someone is caught up in a serious situation, they take everything, and with a firm resolution, return it all to their foundation, where it becomes one and flows as one. This is how we can help not only humans, but also ghosts, animals, and every other kind of being to become unstuck and move forward. This is possible because we are all inherently one, not two.

풀 한 포기나 죽은 사람들까지도 제도하고자 하는 뜻이 있다면 스님이 되세요. 살림하는 사람들은 거기까진 생각을 할 수 없어요. 살기 바빠서 생각이 거기까지 미치지 않아요. 거기에 차이가 있는 것뿐이에요.

사회자: 오늘 큰스님의 높은 법문을 받들다 보니까 어느덧 오늘도 또 예정보다 시간이 많이 경과가 됐습니다. 준비한 질문이 남아 있습니다마는 요다음 법회 날 질문을 드리기로 하고 오늘은 이만 마치면 좋겠습니다.

큰스님: 우리가 마음이 한데 합쳐져서 서로 웃고, 서로 얘기하면서 이렇게 좋은 시간을 보냈습니다. 감사합니다.

So if you want to be a sunim, become a true sunim who can go forth resolutely, spreading awareness of how to rely upon our fundamental mind. Experiencing this true root of ours, this essence of our life, and sharing it with others is the meaning of "Buddhism." If you would be able to help free even dead people and plants, then become a sunim.

People busy with family life are often so caught up in trying to take care of their families that they don't have much time or energy to think about those things. This is the only real difference between sunims and lay people.

Thank you for this wonderful day of sharing and laughing!

한마음출판사의 마음을 밝혀주는 도서

- A Thousand Hands of Compassion
  만가지 꽃이 피고 만가지 열매 익어
  : 대행큰스님의 뜻으로 푼 천수경 (한글/영어)
  [2010 iF Communication Design Award 수상]
- Wake Up And Laugh (영어)
- No River To Cross, No Raft To Find (영어)
- It's Hard To Say (영어) (절판)
- My Heart Is A Golden Buddha (영어)
- Touching The Earth (영어)
- 생활 속의 참선수행 (시리즈) (한글/영어)
  1. 죽어야 나를 보리라
     (To Discover Your True Self, "I" Must Die)
  2. 함이 없이 하는 도리
     (Walking Without A Trace)
  3. 맡겨놓고 지켜봐라
     (Let Go And Observe)
  4. 마음은 보이지 않는 행복의 창고
     (Mind, Treasure House Of Happiness)
  5. 일체를 용광로에 넣어라
     (The Furnace Within Yourself)
  6. 온 우주를 살리는 마음의 불씨
     (The Spark That Can Save The Universe)
  7. 한마음의 위력
     (The Infinite Power Of One Mind)
  8. 일체를 움직이는 그 자리
     (In The Heart Of A Moment)

9. 한마음 한뜻이 되어
   (One With The Universe)
10. 지구보존
    (Protecting The Earth)
11. 진짜 통하게 되면
    (Inherent Connections, 2016 new)
12. 잘 돼야 돼!
    (Finding A Way Forward, 2016 new)
13. 콩씨를 믿는 콩싹
    (Faith In Action, 2016 출판예정)

- 내 마음은 금부처 (한글)
- 건널 강이 어디 있으랴 (한글)
- 처음 시작하는 마음공부1 (한글) (2016 출판예정)
- El Camino Interior (스페인어)
- Vida De La Maestra Seon Daehaeng (스페인어)
- Enseñanzas De La Maestra Daehaeng (스페인어)
- Práctica Del Seon En La Vida Diaria (Colección) (스페인어/영어)
  1. Una Semilla Inherente Alimenta El Universo
     (The Spark That Can Save The Universe)
- Si Te Lo Propones, No Hay Imposibles (스페인어)
- 人生不是苦海 (번체자 중국어) (개정판)
- 无河可渡 (간체자 중국어)
- 我心是金佛 (간체자 중국어) (개정판)

외국출판사에서 출판된 한마음도서

- Wake Up And Laugh
  Wisdom Publications, 미국

- No River To Cross
  (*No River To Cross, No Raft To Find* 영어판)
  Wisdom Publications, 미국

- Wie Fließendes Wasser
  (*My Heart Is A Golden Buddha* 독일어판)
  Goldmann Arkana-Random House, 독일

- Ningún Río Que Cruzar
  (*No River To Cross* 스페인어판)
  Kailas Editorial, S.L., 스페인

- Umarmt Von Mitgefühl
  ('만가지 꽃이 피고 만가지 열매 익어':
  대행큰스님의 뜻으로 푼 천수경 독일어판)
  Diederichs-Random House, 독일

- 我心是金佛
  (*My Heart Is A Golden Buddha* 번체자 중국어판)
  橡樹林文化出版, 대만

- Vertraue Und Lass Alles Los
  (*No River To Cross* 독일어판)
  Goldmann Arkana-Random House, 독일

- Wache Auf Und Lache
  (*Wake Up And Laugh* 독일어판)
  Theseus, 독일

- Дзэн И Просветление
  (*No River To Cross* 러시아어판)
  Amrita-Rus, 러시아

- Sup Cacing Tanah
  (*My Heart Is A Golden Buddha* 인도네시아어판)
  PT Gramedia, 인도네시아

- Không có sông nào để vượt qua
  (*No River To Cross* 베트남어판)
  Phuong Nam Books, 베트남

- *No River To Cross*
  (*No River To Cross* 아랍어판, 제목미상)
  Sphinx Publishing, 이집트 (2016 출판예정)

Books by Daehaeng Kun Sunim
-available through Hanmaum Publications

- Touching The Earth (English) (2015 new)
- A Thousand Hands of Compassion (bilingual, Korean/English)
  [received **2010 iF communication design Award**]
- Wake Up And Laugh (English)
- No River To Cross, No Raft To Find (English)
- My Heart Is A Golden Buddha (English)
- Buddhist Basics (English) (Forthcoming 2016)
- *Practice in Daily Life* (Series) (bilingual, Korean/English)
    1. To Discover Your True Self, "I" Must Die
    2. Walking Without A Trace
    3. Let Go And Observe
    4. Mind, Treasure House Of Happiness
    5. The Furnace Within Yourself
    6. The Spark That Can Save The Universe
    7. The Infinite Power Of One Mind
    8. In The Heart Of A Moment
    9. One With The Universe
    10. Protecting The Earth
    11. Inherent Connections (2016 new)
    12. Finding A Way Forward (2016 new)
    13. Faith In Action (Forthcoming 2016)
- 건널 강이 어디 있으랴 (Korean)
- 내 마음은 금부처 (Korean)
- El Camino Interior (Spanish)
- Vida De La Maestra Seon Daehaeng (Spanish)

- Enseñanzas De La Maestra Daehaeng (Spanish)
- Práctica Del Seon En La Vida Diaria (Series) (bilingual, Spanish/English)
   1. Una Semilla Inherente Alimenta El Universo
- Si Te Lo Propones, No Hay Imposibles (Spanish)
- 人生不是苦海 (Traditional Chinese) (new edition)
- 无河可渡 (Simplified Chinese)
- 我心是金佛 (Simplified Chinese) (new edition)

-Books available through other Publishers

- No River To Cross
  Wisdom Publications, U.S.A.

- Wake Up And Laugh
  Wisdom Publications, U.S.A.

- Wie Fließendes Wasser
  German edition of *My Heart Is A Golden Buddha*
  Goldmann Arkana-Random House, Germany

- Vertraue Und Lass Alles Los
  German edition of *No River To Cross*
  Goldmann Arkana-Random House, Germany

- Umarmt Von Mitgefühl
  German edition of *A Thousand Hands Of Compassion*
  Diederichs-Random House, Germany

- Wache Auf Und Lache
  German edition of *Wake Up And Laugh*
  Theseus, Germany

- Ningún Río Que Cruzar
  Spanish edition of *No River To Cross*
  Kailas Editorial, S.L., Spain

- 我心是金佛
  Traditional Chinese edition of *My Heart Is A Golden Buddha*
  Oak Tree Publishing Co., Taiwan

- Дзэн И Просветление
  Russian edition of *No River To Cross*
  Amrita-Rus, Russia

- Sup Cacing Tanah
  Indonesian edition of *My Heart Is A Golden Buddha*
  PT Gramedia, Indonesia

- Không có sông nào để vượt qua
  Vietnam edition of *No River To Cross*
  Phuong Nam Books, Vietnam

- *No River To Cross* (*title to be determined*)
  Arabic edition of *No River To Cross*
  Sphinx Publishing, Egypt, Forthcoming 2016

한마음선원본원

경기도 안양시 만안구 경수대로 1282(석수동, 한마음선원)
(우편번호 13908)
Tel : 82-31-470-3100 Fax : 82-31-470-3116
홈페이지 : http://www.hanmaum.org
이메일 : jongmuso@hanmaum.org

국내지원

강릉지원 (우)25565 강원도 강릉시 하평5길 29(포남동)
TEL:(033) 651-3003 FAX:(033) 652-0281

공주지원 (우)32522 충청남도 공주시 사곡면 위안양골길 157-61
TEL:(041) 852-9100 FAX:(041) 852-9105

광명선원 (우)27638 충청북도 음성군 금왕읍 대금로 1402
TEL:(043) 877-5000 FAX:(043) 877-2900

광주지원 (우)61965 광주광역시 서구 운천로204번길 23-1(치평동)
TEL:(062) 373-8801 FAX:(062) 373-0174

대구지원 (우)42152 대구광역시 수성구 수성로41길 76(중동)
TEL:(053) 767-3100 FAX:(053) 765-1600

목포지원 (우)58696 전라남도 목포시 백년대로266번길 31-1(상동)
TEL:(061) 284-1771 FAX:(061) 284-1770

문경지원 (우)36937 경상북도 문경시 산양면 봉서1길 10
TEL:(054) 555-8871 FAX:(054) 556-1989

부산지원 (우)49113 부산광역시 영도구 함지로79번길 23-26(동삼동)
TEL:(051) 403-7077 FAX:(051) 403-1077

울산지원 (우)44200 울산광역시 북구 달래골길 26-12(천곡동)
TEL:(052) 295-2335 FAX:(052) 295-2336

제주지원 (우)63308 제주특별자치도 제주시 황사평6길 176-1(영평동)
TEL:(064) 727-3100   FAX:(064) 727-0302

중부경남 (우)50871 경상남도 김해시 진영읍 하계로 35
TEL:(055) 345-9900   FAX:(055) 346-2179

진주지원 (우)52602 경상남도 진주시 미천면 오방로 528-40
TEL:(055) 746-8163   FAX:(055) 746-7825

청주지원 (우)28540 충청북도 청주시 청원구 교서로 109
TEL:(043) 259-5599   FAX:(043) 255-5599

통영지원 (우)53021 경상남도 통영시 광도면 조암길 45-230
TEL:(055) 643-0643   FAX:(055) 643-0642

포항지원 (우)37635 경상북도 포항시 북구 우창로 59(우현동)
TEL:(054) 232-3163   FAX:(054) 241-3503

Anyang Headquarters of Hanmaum Seonwon

1282 Gyeongsu-daero, Manan-gu, Anyang-si,
Gyeonggi-do, 13908, Republic of Korea
Tel: (82-31) 470-3175 / Fax: (82-31) 470-3209
www.hanmaum.org/eng
onemind@hanmaum.org

Overseas Branches of Hanmaum Seonwon

ARGENTINA
Buenos Aires
Miró 1575, CABA, C1406CVE, Rep. Argentina
Tel: (54-11) 4921-9286 / Fax: (54-11) 4921-9286
www.hanmaum.org.ar

Tucumán
Av. Aconquija 5250, El Corte, Yerba Buena,
Tucumán, T4107CHN, Rep. Argentina
Tel: (54-381) 425-1400
www.hanmaumtuc.org

BRASIL
São Paulo
R. Newton Prado 540, Bom Retiro
Sao Paulo, CEP 01127-000, Brasil
Tel: (55-11) 3337-5291
www.hanmaumbr.org

CANADA
Toronto
20 Mobile Dr., North York, Ontario M4A 1H9, Canada
Tel: (1-416) 750-7943
http://www.hanmaum.org/IGateWeb/toronto/index.do

GERMANY
Kaarst
Broicherdorf Str. 102, 41564 Kaarst, Germany
Tel: (49-2131) 969551 / Fax: (49-2131) 969552
www.hanmaum-zen.de

THAILAND
Bangkok
86/1 Soi 4 Ekamai Sukhumvit 63
Bangkok, Thailand
Tel: (66-2) 391-0091
home.hanmaum.org/bangkok

USA
Chicago
7852 N. Lincoln Ave., Skokie, IL 60077, USA
Tel: (1-847) 674-0811
www.buddhapia.com/hmu/chi/

Los Angeles
1905 S. Victoria Ave., L.A., CA 90016, USA
Tel: (1-323) 766-1316
home.hanmaum.org/la

New York
144-39, 32 Ave., Flushing, NY 11354, USA
Tel: (1-718) 460-2019 / Fax: (1-718) 939-3974
www.juingong.org

Washington D.C.
7807 Trammel Rd., Annandale, VA 22003, USA
Tel: (1-703) 560-5166
http://home.hanmaum.org/wa

책에 관한 문의나 주문을 하실 분들은
아래의 연락처로 알려주십시오.

한마음국제문화원/한마음출판사

경기도 안양시 만안구 경수대로 1282 (우)13908
전화: (82-31) 470-3175
팩스: (82-31) 470-3209
e-mail: onemind@hanmaum.org
www.hanmaumbooks.org

If you would like more information about these books or
would like to order copies of them,
please call or write to:

Hanmaum International Culture Institute
Hanmaum Publications
1282 Gyeongsu-daero, Manan-gu, Anyang-si,
Gyeonggi-do, 13908,
Republic of Korea
Tel: (82-31) 470-3175
Fax: (82-31) 470-3209
e-mail: onemind@hanmaum.org
www.hanmaumbooks.org